ROSEBUD ROSES

*Karen ~
What fun we had!
Betty 9-23-18*

Rosebud Roses

Betty Thrasher

ROSEBUD ROSES

Copyright © 2018 Betty Thrasher.

All rights reserved. No part of this book may be used or reproduced by any means, graphic, electronic, or mechanical, including photocopying, recording, taping or by any information storage retrieval system without the written permission of the author except in the case of brief quotations embodied in critical articles and reviews.

iUniverse books may be ordered through booksellers or by contacting:

iUniverse
1663 Liberty Drive
Bloomington, IN 47403
www.iuniverse.com
1-800-Authors (1-800-288-4677)

Because of the dynamic nature of the Internet, any web addresses or links contained in this book may have changed since publication and may no longer be valid. The views expressed in this work are solely those of the author and do not necessarily reflect the views of the publisher, and the publisher hereby disclaims any responsibility for them.

Any people depicted in stock imagery provided by Getty Images are models, and such images are being used for illustrative purposes only.
Certain stock imagery © Getty Images.

ISBN: 978-1-5320-5204-0 (sc)
ISBN: 978-1-5320-5205-7 (e)

Print information available on the last page.

iUniverse rev. date: 07/12/2018

"For many years, Betty Thrasher has been an icon of style and graciousness, as well as a leader and enthusiast of many worthwhile projects in our community.

Betty's book is a vivid, colorful recollection of her life and reflects her great appreciation of life, beauty, integrity, friends and love. It is truly a great gift to her family and friends."

—Sue Mayborn
Publisher
Temple Daily Telegram

"What a fascinating life and entertaining look into small-town America. A real gem!!"

—Robert A. Probe MD
Chief Medical Officer and
Executive Vice President
Baylor Scott and White Health

"In her highly unique, exuberant style and with a phenomenal memory, Betty Thrasher has written an entertaining love letter to her life and to the multitude of characters who've inhabited it. An octogenarian, she retains dazzling energy and a childlike wonder and curiosity that are contagious, uplifting and funny to boot."

—Michael Mullins
Dallas Market Center
Vice President, Public Relations, Marketing and Special Projects
Retired

Betty wearing Aunt Pink's original creation rose petal dress.

DEDICATION

To my beloved family:
Bob, Bobby, Michael, Patti,
Jeffery, Aaron, Tristen and Trevor.

To dear friends in the world of
fashion and our wonderful
customers at The RoseBud.

Especially, I dedicate my thoughts
and appreciation to my parents,
Tommie Little and Harry Monroe Tapman.
And to my brilliant Aunt Rose and Uncle
Sol Cruvand, who were a great influence
on my love for "the store."

With love,
Nana

SUCCESS

To
laugh often and
much; to win the respect
of intelligent people and
affection of children; to earn the
appreciation of honest critics and
endure the betrayal of false friends; to
appreciate beauty, to find the best in
others; to leave the world a bit better,
whether by a healthy child, a garden
patch or a redeemed social condition;
to know even one life has breathed
easier because you have lived.
This is to have succeeded.

—Ralph Waldo
Emerson

CREDITS

1. Louise Chipman knew that I kept a journal so that my children would know about their heritage. She suggested that I write a book.
2. Mary Ann Morton encouraged me to write about my experiences at The RoseBud.
3. Sue Mayborn's advice was especially important to me. She suggested that I publish the book in my handwriting.
4. Ray Reed, commercial printing coordinator for the *Temple Daily Telegram*, devoted much time and thought into the publishing of my book.
5. Henry Skupin, a Rosebud, Texas, native, sent me valuable information on publishing the book. Henry wrote about growing up on the farm. His book was very successful.
6. Dr. Billie Laney, a loyal friend and customer, agreed to critique my material and to offer professional advice. My darling friend was stricken with cancer and passed away before she could read my story.
7. Seleese Thompson shared valuable advice from a business point of view.
8. Valerie Callahan offered to put my words into type.
9. Nancy Birdwell gave me much-welcomed encouragement to write this book. She was a loyal, devoted client of The RoseBud.

10. Michael Mullins thought I had a great story to tell.
11. Matthew Wright found the typist for the first draft.
12. Barbara Chandler and Mary Purifoy called my attention to how much we all grew from our exposure to The RoseBud.
13. Susan Fergus volunteered to help select photos in the book.
14. Celeste Newton offered to type the book. When she became engaged, I knew she would not have the time to do this. In the meantime, Sharon Douglas offered to type these pages. Sharon found Mandy Shelton—who was a blessing to me! Mandy has made it happen! I am so grateful to Sharon and Mandy!

THE ROSE

According to fossil evidence, the rose is thirty-five million years old! The rose most likely came into being in Asia around five thousand years ago! The rose is a phenomenal plant and is rightly known as the world's favorite flower! No other flower has experienced the same popularity!

The rose has been a symbol of love, beauty, even war and politics, from way back in time! The rose comes in a wide variety of colors, sizes and fragrances! The rose is the flower of choice to most—a rose says it all!

My Aunt Rose was a model for the May Company in St. Louis, Missouri, when she and her brilliant husband, Sol Cruvand, came to Rosebud, Texas, as newlyweds to begin a successful business in retail clothing. They were role models to me! I was very close to them!

My Aunt Pink, Elizabeth Little, and her husband, Boston Ford, were very dear to me. They had no children of their own, so I was very special in their lives. Uncle Boss was a meticulous barber at the Roosevelt Hotel in Waco! Aunt Pink was a master seamstress who tried to teach me to sew! This was not one of my interests, so she taught me how to starch and iron men's white dress shirts (which my uncle wore to work every day) and to make the most beautiful and delicious biscuits from scratch! Because of my Aunt Pink, I had beautiful clothes!

My Aunt Johnnye was a fantastic beautician who had a fabulous clientele and no need to take walk-ins! Both Aunt Pink and Aunt Johnnye were my mother's sisters. Johnnye was her twin! Aunt Rose was my dad's older sister! These three aunts had a great impact on my life—I learned so much from each of them! At a very early age, I was very fashion conscious, could cut and style hair and recognize fabrics and good workmanship! My mother was well-groomed, beautiful inside and out and insisted on our looking like the clothing business that our family represented!

My favorite colors were pink and green! The rose was always my favorite flower! My hometown boasted that there was a rosebush in every yard in Rosebud, Texas! So when I solicited my brother's help in naming my first store, it naturally had to be The RoseBud!

Robert Browning said, "It's roses all the way!" I believe this! The rose is very close to my heart, and I am known to buy roses just for me—on a regular basis! My connections with the rose will always bring sweet memories of my mother and the three aunts—Rose, Johnnye and Pink!

How I wish that all of them could have known and been a part of The RoseBud! What a team we would have made! They would have absolutely loved "the store"!

PINK AND GREEN

Box lunch suppers were popular. Girls would decorate their individual boxes in their favorite colors and fill them with delicious food. The box would be auctioned off to the highest bidder. The owner of the box would share dinner with the one who bought her box. My box was always pink and green.

My coloring books were dominated by pink and green. I loved to color, and it was an absolute "no-no" to ever get outside the lines. My pink was a clear, vibrant candy pink—not too bright. My green was lush and beautiful like a well-kept grass yard after a fresh spring rain. These colors have been important to me all my life.

The first RoseBud in Gatesville, Texas, was like a fairytale. The carpet was bright spring green, lush and beautiful. Exotic silk roses proudly graced the store in my favorite shade of candy pink. Soft white walls and ceiling with shiny brass accents were the icing on the cake. I could not believe my eyes! I finally had the wonderful little store I had dreamed of for many years!

When the second RoseBud opened in Temple, Texas, in 1981, the famous green carpet was nowhere to be found, so we had it dyed. The walls were the same soft white, and shiny brass accents were a must. The silk roses grew into an enormous bouquet in various shades of pink, billowing out of Aunt Rose's antique glass fish bowl, firmly planted into an elegant gold-and-patina iron stand. This was the first thing customers saw when they entered the store. This arrangement was proudly displayed on a marble table, a gift from my mother many years before. A huge ornate gold-framed mirror hung in the background. We felt very good that Mother and Aunt Rose were well represented. Oh, how we wished that they could have lived to see The RoseBud!

The RoseBud was warm and inviting! Our customers were comfortable here. When the time came to replace the carpet, we chose a luscious shade of rose, keeping the atmosphere elegant and pleasing. The welcome mat was always out! The cokes were cold, and the coffee was hot, while the champagne was effervescent!

PART I
ROSEBUD, TEXAS

"In character, in manner, in style, in all things,
the supreme excellence is simplicity."

—Henry Wadsworth Longfellow

Betty in her dance costume with Dad.

OPENING

I was born into the clothing business, and I grew up in our stores. I believe that our adult future begins at birth. I was the first child in our family. I always felt especially loved by my parents.

Before I began first grade, my mother enrolled me in Miss Tempie Dunn's expression class. Later, Miss Jean Booth was my speech teacher. Consequently, I have never been at a loss for words or lacked the ability to speak my mind. Miss Veazey, the dance instructor from Waco, came to Rosebud, Texas, twice each week to instill a love for dance in her young students. She left us with rhythm in our bones and a love for tap, ballet and toe dancing. She even threw in a little acrobatics.

My mother must have been an extremely ambitious lady, because it was not long before I was a piano student with Miss Annie Chernoskey. I had no intentions of becoming a concert pianist, so I convinced my parents to purchase this shiny gold E-flat alto saxophone, and I joined the band. My friends and I loved the practice sessions, but we were primarily interested in finding the perfect mate for our handsome band director, Adrian Yett. Our mission was accomplished when he married Jaquelyn Depew. They were made for each other.

In middle school, Mary Jane Sapp and I were majorettes, but in high school, cheerleading was the ultimate. Georgia Marie

Jones, Joe Glen Asbury (the class clown) and I were a real team. We led the Friday night fans at our football games in winning cheers. We always had an outstanding team. I was chosen as head cheerleader, so I guess Miss Tempie's expression class paid off one more time. I am still leading cheers for favorite causes and the town of Rosebud, Texas.

There is a serious story here. Love your children with all your heart. See that they have exposures of a positive nature early on. Be a good example by your own actions and involvements. Praise and encourage them in school. Teach them to seek positive environments in friends and activities. Most important of all, see that they attend Sunday School and church regularly. Teach them to thank God for their many blessings, respect the flag of our United States of America, protect our country and realize how blessed we are to live in the greatest country in the world.

My father, Harry M. Tapman, was a Jew. My mother was an Irish Baptist. My brother, sister and I grew up in the Methodist Church, and it was a very important part of our lives. Religion was never a problem in our family but a great adventure from the beginning.

ARRIVAL IN ROSEBUD

Rose Cruvand's young brother, Harry Monroe Tapman, rode the train from St. Louis to Rosebud, Texas, to learn the trade from his sister and her husband. Sol was a great teacher and an accomplished businessman. Harry was just thirteen years old.

A few years later, Tommie Little, a beautiful, young, blond beauty, came to work at The Leader. Harry was smitten with this talented young lady. They began dating and fell in love. They were married in San Antonio. Tommie Little was born and educated in Rosebud. Her father was a talented blacksmith, Tom or Thomas Little. Her mother was a homemaker. Tommie had a twin sister, Johnnye, but they looked nothing alike.

Tommie and Harry opened their own small-town department store, Harry's Place, in Rosebud, up just one block and across the street from The Leader.

Sol Cruvand was called on by Charlie Brown (bank owner) and Vernon Nicholson (bank president) to save the First National Bank of Rosebud. Sol paid his old friend Fred Florence a visit in Dallas. (Fred Florence was now the president of the bank in which he first swept the floors along with Sol.) The bank loaned Sol the money to insure the bank, so that folks would not withdraw their money. (It was rumored that the bank was in trouble.) The

Betty Thrasher

money Sol borrowed from RNB was loaned to him on his personal signature.

Sol and Charlie Brown greeted the people in front of the bank. Sol personally promised these folks that their money was safe! People trusted and believed in Sol Cruvand. Sol personally repaid the load. In the meantime, he became president of the First National Bank of Rosebud.

When Sol decided to retire from the bank, he agreed to accept land instead of money.

Sol Cruvand became diabetic, had to have one of his legs amputated and died a short time later. (Harry, who had owned five stores in small towns, closed all but Harry's Place when the huge Depression of 1929 hit.) Harry closed his last store in order to go to The Leader to assist Rose. (Uncle Sol had opened the Community Store (hardware, variety and furniture) and Tommie went to work there.)

Rose's and Harry's sister Doris was married to Morris Swartz. They left their shoe store in St. Louis and came to support The Leader. Later, Morris left to return to his shoe store. Doris elected to remain in Rosebud with Rose.

After the deaths of Rose, Doris and Morris, Harry became the sole owner of The Leader. The Community Store closed, and Tommie went back to The Leader to work with Harry. They actually came "full circle"!

Harry eventually sold The Leader after his wife, Tommie, passed away. He came to live at the new retirement center, Canyon Creek, in Temple. He lived here five years before we lost him!

OUR TOWN

Memories of growing up in Rosebud, Texas, are as bright as the sunshine. Those days were filled with happy times and will be forever etched in my mind. I remember how green and fresh the grass looked after a spring rain. Everything was bright and clear, and I was not at all surprised when Ripley said, "Believe it or not: there is a rosebush in every yard in Rosebud, Texas."

The town's motto was: "Everything is Rosy in Rosebud." Truer words were never spoken. This is how I think every Hometown, USA, should be.

As young children we could play outside catching lightning bugs until after dark. We walked everywhere we ventured inside the city limits. Folks left the keys in their cars and never locked their doors. We had great friends from all walks of life. It did not matter how big your house was or what kind of car was in the driveway. We were good people living in the greatest little town in Texas.

Our schools were the best, with outstanding teachers and administrators. Our churches were full of worshipers every time the doors opened. Businesses were thriving. Yards were well kept. Main Street was exciting and inviting. The soda fountain at Buster Lane's Drug Store was the popular place to meet friends. Even Woodland Cemetery was immaculately groomed. Mr. Cone drove his Model T to work there every day to make sure the grounds were perfect. The parks were filled with folks having fun, and the whole town turned out for Friday night football.

Dressing up was just a part of life. Men would not think of going to church without wearing suits and ties. Women would never have worn pants. Folks took great pride in dressing appropriately for the occasion. I am unable to say that any one person wouldn't dare to "outdo" the rest. We had one of these. She only shopped at Neiman Marcus, arrived late to church and sat in the front row. I guess that maybe every small town had one of those ladies.

We return to our town every year in April for the Golden Years Reunion. It is such a thrill to visit with old friends and classmates, sharing stories of our past. We all visit our Rosebud High School Museum in the D Brown Library. We have an exciting program and enjoy a catered dinner. The highlight of the day is the presentation of the Outstanding Alumnus Award. I am proud to say that the first recipient of this prestigious award was my classmate, Thomas Earl Anding. He and his wife, Emmy, gave Baylor University one million dollars, designated for the Mayborn Museum.

Both my brother, Tom Tapman, and I have also received the award.

THE EARLY YEARS

I was born at Providence Hospital in Waco, Texas, on October 3, 1929. I was the first child of Tommie Little and Harry Monroe Tapman, who called Rosebud, Texas, home. My parents owned and operated their small-town department store, Harry's Place. I recall riding my tricycle under the tall tables in the store. My job was to watch and listen. Conversation was for the adults. It was during the Great Depression, and times were hard. People were poor and struggling. I saw a customer put merchandise in the bib of his overalls. I tugged on Dad's pant leg to let him know what I saw. I will never forget the tears in my dad's eyes as he called attention to the situation, saying he would like to make the merchandise a gift. When times were better, the man was still a customer.

As I became a little older, the Main Street sidewalk was my playground, even though I had a huge sand pile under the umbrella of a big chinaberry tree in our backyard. Our home was in the rear of the two buildings that housed our store. I loved playing there, but my favorite pastime was visiting the merchants on our block.

There were some great businesses in our town. I loved climbing the steep steps to the telephone office next door to our store. Della Barlow, a tall, slender, auburn-haired lady was the lone telephone operator. I was mesmerized by Della's beauty and her magic switchboard. (When I was away at college, I called home one evening, and Della came on the line to let me know that my parents were attending a program at the high school and she would tell them I had called.)

Ben Oswalt was a barber at Balhorn's Barber Shop, and he would allow me to finger wave his hair. His wife, Viola, was Dr. Fred Aycock's nurse. Eva Pelham was giving me a lift on her bike when my foot got caught in the spokes of the wheel. Thank goodness, we were right in front of Dr. Aycock's office, and Viola took care of me.

Bravanek's Five-and-Dime store was like a fairyland, and when I had some change, I would spend lots of time deciding what to buy.

Bardin's Cafe was the place to meet. Everyone in town came to drink coffee or eat lunch. Mr. Bardin would ask me to tap dance on the counter for the newcomers to our town. When I was older, the Bardins would clear the dining room and let their kids, Harold and Margie, invite friends to dance to the jukebox. Age was no barrier. We could all join in the fun. All the kids in Rosebud loved to dance. The annual church picnics at Burlington and Westphalia were a natural part of life, and the day always ended with a dance. Besides the delicious food, dancing was considered a very special activity enjoyed by folks of all ages.

The great chinaberry tree and the signature hair ribbon.

THE HOSPITAL EXPERIENCE

My mother insisted that I eat breakfast. Classmate Douglas Ocker playfully tapped me on the head with a book. I was not feeling so good, and soon I felt very sick.

My second-grade teacher, Miss Eulalah Brown, called my mother, and she came to school to pick me up. We went directly to see Dr. Happy Jack Swepston, and since I had a high fever, he admitted me to the hospital. The situation got worse.

It was decided that I had double pneumonia. There were four others in the hospital with the same illness. There were no miracle drugs at this time. We did not even have sulfa drug. I was put in isolation in an oxygen tent.

I spent three and a half months in the Swepston Hospital under the care of Dr. Swepston and Dr. Joe Harrell, who was on leave from the army. The doctors were devastated. They called Dr. Walter Smith from Marlin to come over for a consultation. The three doctors decided to remove a rib and drain my lungs. Because I had pneumonia, they would not be able to put me to sleep for the surgery. I would have to endure a local anesthesia. My mother was allowed to go into surgery with me. She put cotton in my ears so that I would not hear the sounds and the conversations.

In the meantime, one by one, the four adult pneumonia patients passed away. I was not aware of this, but our Methodist minister, Dr. Durwood Blackwell, was holding daily prayer vigils on my behalf. All of Rosebud was sending up prayers for me. God surely heard them, and He passed me over.

A handsome high school senior, the son of Dr. Fred Aycock, was stopping by the hospital every day to tell me a story. He was probably the most popular young man in town, and he was unselfishly devoting time each day to a little eight-year-old kid who was so very sick. T.P. Aycock was a young lieutenant in the United States Army when he lost his life in combat. What a loss!

My Aunt Rose and Uncle Sol were such wonderful people in my life. All during the long hospital stay, I craved my favorite foods: tomatoes and strawberries. These fruits did not really go together but were at the top of my list, and no one could guarantee that I would live. The Cruvands sent crates of tomatoes and strawberries on a regular basis—enough to share with all the patients and employees. I ate so many strawberries and tomatoes that I broke out in a rash. I just kept on eating them until the rash gave up. Orange Crush soda was the other item that I loved. Uncle Sol Cruvand made it his first concern to see that we had Orange Crush galore!

Most of the time, in my delirium, I wished for the most unusual items, like sandals with Snow White and the Seven Dwarfs on them. My dad had white sandals in our store and convinced a local artist to paint these characters on the sandals.

I begged for a beautiful bright-green dress with white polka dots. Of course, my sweet Aunt Pink took this request very seriously, and before it was humanly possible, the dress appeared and hung itself on the closet door so I could see it all day long.

Every day, nurse Helen Cooper would come down the hall in her immaculately starched white uniform. You could hear the rustle of the fabric from quite a distance, and I always wondered if that perfectly starched uniform was really comfortable…or was this what made her so irritable! She would enter my room with a huge needle, and I would put up my best defenses in order to avoid this hurtful incident. I warned her that I would tell Dr. Swepston what she was doing to me. So when he made his rounds one day, I cried huge tears and pleaded for him to do away with this awful needle. He honored my request by asking Nurse Helen to bring the needle to my room to put on the mantel among my many other prized possessions and promised that I would never, ever get stuck with that old needle again!

I loved that mantel with all my special treasures and the beautiful green-and-white polka-dot dress on the door. When I was much better, I had absolutely no recollection of making any of the requests.

As I think back on this crucial time in my life, I wonder how my darling mother survived. She had a brand-new baby girl about two months old, a little five-year-old son and an eight-year-old in the hospital for three and a half months. No doubt about it, Tommie Little Tapman was a strong woman!

The day of my dismissal from Swepston Hospital was a celebration.

THE WHITE SUITS

When Dr. Walter Smith came from Marlin, Texas, to confer with Drs. Swepston and Harrell concerning my illness, he always wore a white suit with a red rose at his lapel. His snow-white hair and mustache were so perfect for the outfit. I loved for him to visit.

Then, one day, right out of the blue, this striking Hollywood movie star just strolled right into my hospital room! He was wearing his gorgeous white western outfit with leather fringe, a ten-gallon hat and white western boots! My heart skipped a beat, and I could not believe my eyes! This was my very favorite movie star, Tom Mix! (I wondered if I had gone to heaven.)

Rosebud, Texas, was honored to have such a prominent guest. Tom Mix was the nephew of Hortense Harrell, Dr. Joe Harrell's wife! I was a very lucky little girl to have so many folks go that extra mile for me!

CLASSMATES

We started first grade together and graduated from high school in 1947. We were a close-knit group, and I have very fond memories of these friends. Mary Jane Sapp, Georgia Marie Jones, Rosemary Tucker and Billie Jean Vlha were my closest friends. Jane Ruth (Bootsie) Williams, Annie Ruth Summers and Aline Wieser were an inseparable threesome. Anne Weatherby and Betty Jean Gummelt moved into Rosebud later but were very much a part of our group. In our town, we were all very good friends.

Thomas Earl Anding, John R. Killgore Jr., John Eldon Curtis, John William Schigut, Cecil Newton Goodman, George Barlow, Joe Glen Asbury, William (Cookie) Goeke, Douglas Ocker, Jimmy Lemley, Ernest Hrozek and Bill Lierman were an outstanding group. Later, we were blessed to welcome P.J. Hoelcher, Frank Voltin, Leonard Stermer, Bill Heck, Robert Lee Schuetze, Lloyd Stoebner, Ogene Pomykal, Jimmy Litzman, Billy Van Davis and Bill Gaylor. Monroe Parcus and George Cruz were among the originals.

More girls began to join us when Helen Jo Olbrich, Doris Schneider, Eileen Petrek, LaVern Zipperlin, Joanne Doree, June Asbury, Frances Cabron, Wanda Blakely, Marceline Zavodney and Doris Hejl grew our group even larger.

All of us worked together on committees or in different

organizations. Many were active in various sports. Senior class officers were: Doug Ocker, president; Jane Sapp, secretary; Frank Voltin, vice president; George Barlow, treasurer; and Leonard Stermer, monitor. Whatever the occasion was to bring us together, we had loads of fun.

In the summers, all the boys worked either in family businesses, baling hay, delivering newspapers or at various service stations. But George Barlow was the famous chemist. His laboratory put our school's lab in the shade. In fact, the chemistry class often went to George's lab for serious experiments until…he blew it up! His time was totally spent putting his lab back in operation. George was a fine Christian. His favorite book was the Bible. George became an executive in a very prominent chemical company. George died before our thirty-fifth RHS reunion. It was not as much fun without him.

Many of these friends have passed away. Those of us left behind miss them terribly. Our annual Rosebud High School Golden Years Reunion, held every April, will never be the same without them. They will not be forgotten.

Among these groups, one could count on a wide range of talent in many areas: medicine, athletics, music, song, dance, literature, education, farming, law and business. We loved getting together, and we never needed a specific reason, because when the class of 1947 was in place, it was like a celebration. The only thing lacking was fireworks.

MY FIRST TRIP TO MARKET

This was my first trip to market, and I was bursting with excitement. I was only six years old, and just Dad and I were going to the shoe market in Dallas. I was quick to develop a passion for shoes. To this day, I love high-heeled shoes because they are much more flattering, and if one is short, like me, heels make us look and feel tall.

I have been attending market in Dallas for more than eighty years. It is such a part of my life, and I love seeing special friends. They always make me feel welcome, even though I no longer have my wonderful store. It is an eerie feeling not having a store, because someone in our family always had one. I am sad to say that I am the one to end this tradition.

My business allowed me to meet so many interesting and talented folks. Every day was a new adventure, and yes, I would do it all over again!

When I was at market, I tried to take in all the sights. There were so many exciting showrooms offering different types of fashion. One could spend hours just researching the many options.

During the Rosebud days, we concentrated mostly on clothes for the entire family, some household items and shoes. Fabrics and piece goods were a huge part of our business because most ladies sewed clothes for the family. Threads, laces, tapes, buttons, hooks and eyes, ribbons and all the various trimmings were very

Rosebud Roses

important. I always managed to attend a gift-wrapping class. Our store offered free gift wraps to our customers, and we did not spare any punches. Our wraps were gorgeous.

There was a special bond between store owners and the folks who shopped with them. First these people were our friends, and then they were our customers.

My dad offered credit to the customers. If there was a crisis, and the crops did not come in as successfully as expected, he carried the debts until the customer was able to pay.

Bubba is three years old and Betty is six years old.

WE WERE CAMP FIRE GIRLS

All through our years together, our group was seriously involved with Camp Fire. We spent summer sessions at Camp Tonkawa in Crawford, Texas. The country was so beautiful, and our imaginations seemed to get the best of us as we thought about the Native American tribes who must have lived and died on this land.

I remember a huge waterfall on the property, where we used to swim and earn water awards. Rafting and canoeing were fun, but my favorite outing was an overnight campout on horseback. We built big campfires and slept under the stars. We learned to fry an egg on a rock and to make delicious stew over hot coals in deep holes. Coffee boiled in a tin can was delicious.

I remember my counselors so well. They made big impressions on us. Bess Hyronemus was from Temple. Jean Ann Madeley was also from Temple. Joanne Mason lived in Waco. These young ladies were a very special breed, and the campers adored them!

Many years later, when I was a grandmother, my friend Liza and I took little Jeffery Todd Thrasher to Camp Tonkawa to see the big, beautiful waterfall and to tell him stories about our Camp Tonkawa experiences. We were speechless to find a very small, trickling waterfall—nothing like we remembered. Jeffy looked at us and said, "This waterfall is *not* big!" Time changes things.

Nevertheless, we had all been faithful to our days as Camp

Fire Girls. We loved our leader, Carol Souther, and treasured our visits to Salado Creek.

During our high school years, we organized a Camp Fire Social Club and gave it a Greek name: Sigma Alpha Sigma. We sent formal invitations to our social events and requested written replies. The boys did not like to write notes to accept or decline, but they learned a thing or two that some of them would never have learned from home.

The bottom line is that we had good times and brushed up on our etiquette. Laura Lane Parks and I were the leaders of the Horizon Club.

Betty, Rosemary, Jane and Georgia—friends
from first grade to the bitter end.

MY TENTH BIRTHDAY

I especially remember my tenth birthday. We thanked God for my complete recovery from that awful illness. Our family was finally getting back to normal, everyday life. My little sister, Peggy Sue, was two years old, and we were all so proud of her. What an adorable age!

We lived in a new house about two blocks from the store, and everyone was happy. This is the year that I got my wonderful Story & Clark upright piano for my tenth birthday.

Christmas morning brought a shiny new bicycle, and hanging on its handle was a breathtaking pink silk charmeuse lounging pajama set created by my Aunt Pink! Things were really rosy in Rosebud long before the slogan was adopted by our town!

PIANO RECITAL

This was the year our piano recital took place in the Rosebud High School auditorium. My entire family was present for this big event! The teacher was Miss Annie Chernoskey, who was quite accomplished in this field and had studied in Europe.

I had practiced diligently and felt that I was well rehearsed. I took my seat at the piano on the huge stage and began to play my assigned selection. Halfway through the performance, I drew a complete blank and could not remember another note! After five serious attempts to continue, I located my mother's face in the audience. The minute I laid eyes on her, it all came back to me. I finished my performance with a flourish! Miss Annie, who was very stern and serious, gave me a little smile! This was the reward!

The moral of this story is that we never want to disappoint our precious mothers! And persistence always wins.

OUR MOVIE STAR

Bootsie's little cousin was a star in *Our Gang* comedies. He was the chubby little boy called Spanky, who always wore a skull cap. He had the cutest face! When he came to Rosebud to visit his Grandmother Williams, we would get a crowd together and walk all over town. We loved showing off our movie star, and of course, each of us had a skull cap.

Mrs. Billy Williams lived in a huge house with a wrap-around porch. Bootsie invited us to spend the night on many occasions. We loved sleeping in her wonderful feather beds and waking up to the delicious smell of homemade doughnuts. This house could have told many great stories. As a girl, my mother said she learned to smoke grapevine under the same bush in this yard. We loved this story.

The Williams family had many really beautiful girls. Bootsie's mother was one of them. They all favored each other. One of them, Ruby Rogers, worked at The Leader.

UP AND DOWN ROSEBUD'S MAIN STREET

We had many good people in Rosebud, Texas. I remember them so well because each one had some sort of impact on my life.

Ourn Sapp kept yards beautifully manicured. His wife was a sweet lady who sewed for the public.

Dick Depew was the cotton buyer.

Joe Vlha and Richard Conner were the tax men.

Grady Wright delivered groceries and raised greyhound dogs.

Dr. L.A. Trubee was a dentist who also delivered the *Dallas Morning News*.

Dr. E.H. O'Neil was a dentist who loved to hunt.

Dr. Johnson was the veterinarian.

Drs. Swepston, Harrell and Wheelis kept us healthy at the Swepston Hospital.

Dr. Halbert came to run the new hospital.

Mr. Kirksey owned the Gem Theatre.

Mose Hill was a rancher and, later, our constable.

Carl and Minnie Butler owned the fabulous El Tampico Mexican Restaurant.

Johnny Plasek flipped the best hamburgers.

Mrs. Nicholson owned Nicholson Funeral Home.

Clarence Hoelscher was her friendly undertaker.

John Green owned Green's Funeral Home.

Marshall, his son, was the undertaker.

Frances Wheelis Tarver looked like Rosalind Russell.

Nonie Wrinn loved beautiful clothes.

Mozelle Nicholson only shopped at Neiman's.

Dell Kalfus was Hank Thompson's aunt.

Hortence Harrell was Tom Mix's aunt.

Raleigh Sapp played sports at the University of Texas. He also had a cotton gin.

Winnie Sapp was a very special lady.

Jackie and Jiggs Walston owned a florist and jewelry store.

Donald and Annie Ruth Glass were owners of Glass the Florist.

Royce Jackson was Mr. Agriculture.

Bully Gillstrap assisted Dana X. Bible at UT.

Joe Smilie was a polished gentleman–rancher. Kathleen was a precious petite lady.

Robert and Sim Souther had Souther's Super Market.

Lorene Parcus made delicious cookies.

Hilton Haupt was Mr. Electricity.

Roma Lee Haupt was a lady in the know.

Dick Tucker, A.L. Freeman and Luther Parks headed up Rural Electric Company at different times.

Gene Schmidt, cotton gin owner.

Richard, Wright and Claud Ellison were very prominent ranchers.

Chandler Hargrove, Allis Chalmers Farm Equipment.

Voltin Chevrolet later became…

Lee Ray McAtee Chevrolet.

Ray McAtee Ford Dealership.

Bert Thrasher, Gulf Oil and Pontiac Dealer.

Henry Lamar, George Stock, Wm. Cone, LeRoy Baca and Bo Dorset were lumberyard men.

Judge J.R. Glass's Magnolia Station had the flying red horse.

Lorene Harris's Beauty Shop was our *Steel Magnolias*.

Rosebud Roses

Jamie Cunningham's Drive-In was the popular place to meet after work.

Dicia Tarver loved red lipstick and never wore hose.

Lillian Skinner had a decided Southern drawl.

Georgia Bethel was a beautiful, gracious lady.

Mrs. Sam Henslee was so pretty and looked like Myrna Loy, the movie star.

Mary Ligon and Winnie Sapp were elegant ladies and were sisters, whom everyone loved.

Helen Cooper was a very good nurse.

Charlie Collins was a barber and a Church of Christ lay minister.

Mrs. Brooks owned the beauty salon where my Aunt Johnnye worked.

Lena Lynn cooked good kosher food in their store.

John T. Canipe owned an upscale men's clothing shop. George Ocker worked the tailor shop.

Ikie Kahler and sons owned a men's clothing store and a tailor shop.

Ernestine Green, daughter of Mr. and Mrs. E.E. Green, was personal secretary to Congressman W.R. (Bob) Poage in Washington, D.C.

Charlie Brown, prominent rancher and banker.

Chester Anding, Sinclair consignee.

Millard Ligon, Texaco consignee and cotton gin.

Paul Reichert, Humble Oil consignee.

M.L. and Cecil Light, dry cleaners.

Earl Jones, Magnolia consignee.

J.R. Kilgore, post master and *Rosebud News*.

Vera Warrock family, *Rosebud News*.

Everette Beards, post master.

Ira Stallworth, US mail carrier.

Sol Cruvand, president First National Bank and merchant.

J.A. Tarver Sr., president Planters National Bank.

Betty Thrasher

J.A. Tarver II, Planters National Bank.

J.A. Tarver III, Planters National Bank and Republic National of Dallas.

Jack Tarver, Planters National Bank.

Raymond Brod, grocer.

Walter Wrinn, grocer.

Pete Bubella, grocer.

Tom Cruse, grocer.

Edward Flores, grocer.

John C. Green, grocer.

John C. Green Jr., grocer.

E.A. Birkelbach, grocer.

Paul Zipperlin, drive-in grocery.

M.A. Belson, drug store, pharmacy.

Buster Lane, drug store, pharmacy.

Charles and Lillian Monroe, drug store, pharmacy.

Sam Henslee, hardware store.

Sam and Lillian Skinner, hardware store.

Rose and Sol Cruvand, The Leader, Cruvands.

Harry M. Tapman, Harry's Place, The Leader.

Sol Cruvand, The Famous, Community Store.

Tommie Tapman, Harry's Place, Community Store.

A.D. Whitfield Sr., wrecking yard.

A.D. Whitfield Jr., Washington Redskins.

Clarence Boyd, fine auto doctor.

Wilbur Johnson, entertaining mechanic.

Nelson Malcik, furniture store.

Ed Malcik, Five and Dime Store.

Bravenec's, Five and Dime Store.

J.I. Bardin, City Cafe.

John Placek, short-order diner.

El Tampico, fine Mexican cuisine.

Bienhauer Bakery, Tony and Margaret.

Dairy Queen on Highway 77.
Beckers City Cafe.
Balhorn Barber Shop.
Balhorn Beauty Shop.
Brooks Beauty Shop.
M.E. Jones, RHS Superintendent.
J.W. Baker, RHS Principal.
LBJ Sikes, football coach at RHS.
A.O. Bowen, RHS superintendent.
L.A. Holmes, RHS superintendent.
W.A. Ferguson, RHS principal.
T.R. Mobley, RHS principal.
Chester Richerson, football coach.
Glen Lowe, RHS football coach.
Adrian L. Yett, band master.
Martha Brogden, band director.

Betty, Jeanie and June with Daddy in the ladies' section of Harry's Place.

WORKING AT THE STORE

I worked in the stores after school and on Saturdays. It was my job to dress the store windows. I loved this assignment, and I let the creative juices flow. Aunt Rose would say, "Betty, please do not put our most expensive items in the windows." I overruled and sure enough, they were the first to sell. It was also my job to do the grocery shopping on Saturday morning for Mother and Aunt Rose. It also meant that I would deliver my purchases to both houses and put the items away. Then I was expected to report to the store for work. Saturdays were our busiest days.

My friends often went to the movies on Saturday afternoons, but I worked at the store, and it just did not seem fair. At home, I was expected to share in all the chores. Mother thought it was important to know how to cook, and I was a fast learner. I babysat my little brother and sister and chauffeured my Aunts Rose and Dora, who didn't drive. And last, there was the work at the stores. You might say that I was well rounded. At our house, no one left until the jobs were done, and we each had our assignments.

The moral to this story is that when I married and had a home and children of my own, I was very capable of handling the job. I have thanked my parents hundreds of times for grooming me for life's responsibilities.

OUTSTANDING HOMES

We were proud of the homes in our town. Some were very small and really unnoticeable, but most yards were very well kept. Then there were those spacious homes of the more affluent that we thought of as the masterpieces of our small town.

THE HENSLEE HOME

The Henslee home stood proud and tall among the more modest ones in its neighborhood. This two-story creation was painted in pale yellow and blue tones with artistic carvings enhancing the outside. This family had three children: Sam, J.T. and Hannah.

I shall never forget Hannah's wedding to C.B. Searcy in the beautiful rose garden. This was quite an event. All the guests arrived dressed in their best finery. It was a very fashionable occasion. The home was the perfect setting.

Later, this great home belonged to the Raleigh Sapp family. They had a daughter, Mary Jane, and a son, David. The lady of the house, Winnie Wells Sapp, was a gracious, well-educated lady admired by all of us. She was as beautiful within as she was on the surface. And she was the mother of my friend, Jane, who was maid of honor in our wedding. Our rehearsal dinner was in the magnificent dining room. This was a gift from the Sapp family.

The Tarver Home

The stately brown-brick home of the John Albert Tarver Sr. family stood two stories tall. Mrs. Tarver, Jessie Grace, was reflected in the tasteful rooms of this mansion. The Tarvers had two sons, John Albert Jr. and Jack. Mrs. Tarver was a tiny, petite little woman. She was very attractive and dressed beautifully. It was obvious that she had very good taste.

John Jr. married beautiful Lillie, and they had a son, John Albert III. When Lillie died in San Antonio, her husband and little son returned to Rosebud for John to join his father at the family-owned Planters National Bank. Later, John married Dicia, and they had two children, Bill and Gayle. Both John Jr. and Jack served their country in the United States Army.

Jack married Frances Wheelis, who I thought looked like the movie star Rosalind Russel. Jack served his army time in the South Pacific. As he was preparing to come home, he drowned while swimming. Frances and his two small children, Grace and Jack, were anxiously awaiting his return in their beautiful new yellow-brick home.

The J.R. Glass and H.J. Swepston Homes

Judge and Mrs. J.R. Glass lived on the far end of Rosebud's Main Street in one of two identical white-frame two-story homes. Dr. and Mrs. H.J. Swepston lived in the other home next door. These two impressive homes stood guard over the affluent neighborhood. The yards were impeccably manicured.

When Bob and I announced our engagement, hostesses Winnie Sapp, Dicia Tarver, Lorene Swepston and Mrs. Glass entertained us with a lovely tea shower in the Glass home. I was overwhelmed! This was an elegant party, and we were absolutely speechless.

THE FREEMAN HOME

The stately Freeman home was located two blocks off Main Street. Ruth Freeman Summers grew up here as a young girl. This home is a landmark in our town because it was eventually converted into Dr. Happy Jack Swepston's Hospital. It was later renovated into a magnificent private home. Today, my good friend, Judge Matthew Wright, is the proud owner. With Matthew living there, the lights have come on again in this beautiful home. It is a real credit to Rosebud!

I spent three and a half months here, as a child, with double pneumonia, an illness that few survived. Judge Wright has designated my room, from long ago in the hospital, as the Betty Ann Room. It is impeccably decorated and furnished with the best! I feel so honored.

In 2014, Matthew opened his warm, friendly home to all the ex-students of Rosebud High School who were attending the Annual Golden Years Reunion. We brought 319 visitors to the house that day. Delightful refreshments were served to all the guests who toured the home. The host provided a register with space for a brief account of each guest's experience at Swepston Hospital.

I felt especially honored that my dear friend, Judge Wright, opened his home to us on this special day of the RHS Golden Years Reunion 2014. It was such a generous treat for all of us in attendance. Judge Matthew Wright's law office is located on Rosebud's Main Street.

THE JOE VLHA HOME

One of the homes in Rosebud that means the most to me is the Joe Vlha home. This was not a mansion in terms of size, but it was a castle to me because of the folks who lived there. Joe and Luna Raabe Vlha had three daughters: Joyce, Mary Jo and Billie

Jean. I spent so much time here that it was like a second home. Luna made me feel like one of her girls.

This mother was loaded with so many talents. She was a small person who accomplished big things. One time when I spent the night with Jeanie on a school night, we arrived home after school the next day to find that Luna had papered the walls of the girls' bedroom and had sewn new drapes and hung them on the windows. Soon after, she created new spreads and bed skirts. The modest house was beautiful and happy. It could have been an advertisement in a magazine. This was a friendly house that welcomed us with open arms.

MIDDLE SCHOOL

Mrs. Ruby Nichols Binns was our seventh-grade English teacher. She was brilliant. I loved watching her stand before our class, dressed in long, narrow skirts and tailored silk blouses belted to perfection at her small waist. All the girls wanted to look like her. She wore her strawberry blonde hair in a short style, tucked behind her ears to emphasize the tortoise horn-rimmed glasses that were her trademark.

Mrs. Binns was a stickler for perfection. She had two grades in her classroom: zero and one hundred. If a student scored a zero, he or she would stay after school for as many days as it took to earn the one hundred mark. Not one of us left her class with a zero average. We were probably the smartest group in the history of Rosebud schools. Mrs. Binns had the patience of Job, but she only expected and demanded the best from her students.

Our class chose the colors of red, white and blue for our promotion program into high school. Our song was, "When the Lights Go on Again (All Over the World)." Jane Sapp and I were the pianists. Aunt Pink assisted all the seamstresses in making the girls' outfits. We wore navy silk pebble crepe stitched-down pleated skirts and white eyelet surplus wrap blouses with short puff sleeves and peplums. Our belts were red grosgrain fabric with self-covered buckles.

The boys wore white trousers, white long-sleeved dress shirts, navy blazer jackets and red silk ties. We all felt pretty sharp. Mrs. Binns was proud of us.

Middle school, as a whole, was very exciting and filled with adventurous events. We were kind of sad to leave these early times and advance into the world of unknowns in high school. This meant that we were growing up and leaving behind our younger years.

School was out, and summer came. We packed lunches and pedaled our bikes to our secret playground at the edge of town. We pricked our fingers and claimed our fame as blood sisters 'til death. We traded stories of the utmost confidence and swore secrecy. (I still cannot remember what was so top secret). We were understandably sad when it was time to bicycle home and return our thoughts to real life.

Our end-of-the-year seventh grade picnic was loads of fun. We could not help but feel that a precious time in our lives was coming to a close. We were discussing the pros and cons of years gone by when I was encouraged to hop on a picnic table and perform my famous imitation of Mrs. Binns in her classroom. I was well into the part where Mrs. Binns would shift from one side to the other with a twist of her hips as she unconsciously popped her girdle. Suddenly, the laughter ceased, and it was unusually quiet. Mrs. Binns had arrived and was standing behind me with her hands on her hips and an unpleasant look on her face. She firmly demanded that I repeat the whole performance once more while facing her dead-on! I was never so humiliated. When my mom recalled the incident and asked for an explanation, I said, "It is probably Miss Tempie's fault for teaching me to always express myself."

Mrs. Binns will forever own a special place in my heart. She was among my favorite teachers, and I had quite a few. In her later years, she lost her eyesight. When folks invited her to ride to Temple for a visit to The RoseBud, she would respond with a beautiful smile and happily accept the invitation. I can still see this darling lady sitting on the sofa and saying, "Betty Ann, this store looks just like you."

Ruby Binns was a fabulous teacher with loads of energy. She was a stickler for diagramming sentences. She expected her students to use proper English, speak clearly, use perfect diction and to stand up straight. She spent endless hours teaching us to develop good handwriting skills. She used verses to describe the parts of speech, such as, "Interjections show surprise, such as 'Oh, how pretty' and 'Ah, how wise!'"

Ruby Binns would have been so proud of The RoseBud fashion shows. She was a beautiful person who appreciated beautiful things. When my first full-page advertisement appeared in *Ultra* magazine, with photos of my daughters-in-law dressed in gorgeous Oscar de la Renta dresses and Alexis Kirk jewelry, I went to see Mrs. Binns and left her a copy. I knew that she could see it in spite of her handicap, and of course, she thought the ad was absolutely gorgeous.

Our early years were blessed with great teachers in every class, and I can honestly say that all of them were my true friends all through life.

Ruby Binns died at age ninety-five but will always live in my memories.

ROSEBUD HIGH SCHOOL

Byron Stubbs, the local Boy Scout Master, was an electrician by trade. He was also a skilled photographer, and at the first sign of bluebonnets in the spring, we headed to the Rosebud City Lake to be captured on film in the fields of blue.

Byron made a point of photographing special times and places for Rosebud kids. We wondered how he could be in so many places at a given time. We found the answer to our question when we graduated or got married. Byron would present each of us with a precious little red box, carefully constructed by his talented hands. Inside the box were many colorful slides of important times and places meaningful to each individual. A small viewer was also inside the box filled with life's best memories. This was a precious gift from one who played a major role in our formative years. What a gift!

Our senior English teacher, Mary Lee, was a spinster until she and Byron Stubbs met, fell in love and married. Mrs. Stubbs was a huge fan of William Shakespeare. The main feature in her English classroom was a bust of this gentleman. One of her requirements was that we memorize Chaucer in *olde* English. At a recent reunion of RHS Golden Years, one of our own, Robert Arthur, suggested we adopt Chaucer as the official password of Rosebud High School. The motion was unanimously accepted.

Rosebud Roses

We probably spent more time on the study of English literature than any other subject. Mrs. Stubbs, we were sure, did not even know there *was* another subject. She was our class sponsor and coach of the one-act play. So there was no doubt that we excelled in this undertaking. These were fun times. Our group auditioned for parts, and most of us were selected for our senior and one-act play performances.

In Rosebud, the children were everyone's business. We were well cared for and expected to have good manners and impeccable morals. We were taught responsibility seriously. Rosebud's reputation was dependent on our actions, and not one of us wanted to muddy the water.

There were so many different groups of friends in our midst. Frances Cone, Ann Longmoor, Rosemary Ligon, June Linn and Patsy Smilie were a couple of years older. Our bunch thought these girls were cool.

The War years had a great impact on us. We knew what it was like to have food, shoes and gasoline rationed. We were taught to be ultraconservative and not waste anything.

Rosebud was blessed with fine people. It was difficult to send our young men off to war, but our country was proud and free and must be protected in order to keep it safe and sound. Some of our boys were drafted, while others rushed to volunteer upon graduation from high school. America was worth fighting for. Volunteering was easy to do—our USA was well worth whatever we must do.

Our guys and girls (nurses) were sent all over the world. Some never got a leave to come home. Many lost their lives and would never return. T.P. Aycock, the handsome high school senior who visited me in the hospital every day to tell stories (when I was just eight years old), was a bright young lieutenant in the US Army when he lost his life.

Handsome Jack Tarver was a young army officer in the South Pacific, about to be shipped home, when he drowned in an accident. It was a very sad time in Rosebud when we lost Jack Tarver. He was Rosebud's fair-haired son, a wonderful, kind and compassionate young man, and he was my special friend. Jack had been a pallbearer for my Uncle Sol's funeral. The war was costly, and every town and city in America felt these losses.

Rosebud was represented by several church denominations. Baptist and Catholic churches were among the most prominent. Our good friends, Cecil Goodman and Gene Linn, and their families were devout members of the Church of Christ. Probably, the largest representation was supported by the Catholics.

Church was highest on everyone's list. I loved our beautiful First Methodist Church, which faced the corner of Main Street. I never missed Sunday School and Methodist Youth Fellowship. At one time, I taught the primary class and then played the organ at the Lutheran Church. I dreamed of having all our weddings in the circular sanctuary of First Methodist. This was our most beautiful building, designed and built by Jane's grandfather.

Our family treasured our black friends. We always attended their football games and special revival services at their church. My dad ordered fabrics in bright green and white for the band, majorettes and cheerleaders. I especially remember the football star we called Dynamite. Their team was the Wilson White Lions.

Our school could not afford leather athletic jackets to award our boys, so they received beautiful black sweaters with that prestigious gold chenille letter on the front.

They asked if I would print the annual. I'm sure I was selected because of Mrs. Ruby Binns' insistence I master her requirements in seventh grade. I printed the 1947 Rosebud annual in black India ink on graph paper with a pen staff. It turned out surprisingly well.

Rosebud Roses

My good friend, chemist and talented artist George Barlow, did the artwork.

When we graduated, our class boasted sixty-nine members. We were one of the largest classes to attend RHS. We also brought about more changes than any other class. We were known for speaking our minds.

It was against the rules to dance at school. Well, it was obvious that our senior prom would include dancing. I remember personally visiting each member of the school board and asking for this rule to be lifted. If not, we would take our prom to the Red Circle, a popular nightclub in Barclay. We secretly called the establishment the "Bloody Bucket." I do not recall how we came up with this name, never having been inside the place.

Our classmate, John R. Kilgore Jr., had a solution. His family owned the *Rosebud News*. So we went to the news office and printed circulars stating our plan. We hand-delivered these circulars to every home and business in town. We were told that the local Baptist church had petitioned "no dancing in the school" fifty years before. We were thrilled to be in the group to see this petition reversed. The party was an enormous success. We spent weeks choosing the perfect attire. Beauty shops were overflowing on the day of the prom. Everyone was gorgeous, and we conducted ourselves like our town expected us to. We had talented Baylor University students to present a fabulous show and music for dancing. We did put a system in place. Should anyone decide to leave after the required sign-in procedure, they would not be allowed to come back inside.

These wonderful high school years were filled with hard work, school activities, love of life and dedication to our town.

THE YELLOW CATALINA SWIMSUIT

One of my most treasured gifts for graduation from RHS was a gorgeous hand-painted Catalina swimsuit! This was the ultimate prize! During the war, this swimsuit was among a precious cargo of merchandise that had been stored in railroad cars! (Folks were not interested in using their hard-earned money for such luxuries!) I could hardly contain my excitement when I would wear this treasure for the first time! Did I tell you the suit was yellow? Our group drove to Cameron for a swim party! I was no Esther Williams, but I felt beautiful in my glamorous Catalina! When I jumped into the pool, the suit disintegrated, and needless to say, I was humiliated! Because my friends immediately came to the rescue, I was able to survive! I never really cared much for swimming after that!

THE OLD RHS BUILDING

Our prestigious brown-brick Rosebud High School building should have been a monument to our town, had it been saved. Many workable reasons could have been put to use inside this stately landmark, such as city offices, a library and a museum. A world of other ideas could have kept this wonderful building alive. This ground, where the magnificent Rosebud High School once stood, remains empty and unproductive on our Main Street. We miss this beautiful building.

The Golden Years Reunion group, under the leadership of Gene Linn, did erect a very small memorial on this property to recognize and honor those who paid the ultimate price in the service of our country during World War II. The monument also recognizes those who receive the Outstanding Alumnus Award.

Among the most cherished mementos of school years gone by were large framed photos of each graduating class, members of the administration and the class officers. Each frame represented the year of graduation for every year the school was active. I was told these treasured photos would have been destroyed when the building was taken down if Jack and John Kilgore had not saved them. Today, these fabulous class treasures proudly hang on the walls of our RHS Museum in the D Brown Library of Rosebud, Texas.

Betty Thrasher

When Rosebud and Lott schools merged, new buildings were constructed in Travis, the halfway distance from each of the two towns. The school mascot is the cougar.

Buildings are just buildings, but the Rosebud High School ex-students, the folks who walked the halls of our beloved school, are the real reason to celebrate. We're the Rosebud Black Panthers, and every one of us will have a soft spot in our hearts for having been a part of the history of dear ole Rosebud High. We will never outgrow these precious memories.

OFF TO COLLEGE

While growing up, I set my sights on attending Texas A&M. However, it was not a coeducational school when I was ready for higher learning. So I made the plan to attend Texas Tech in Lubbock. I was sure that this would place me far enough away that I would not be called home to work on those busy Saturdays.

I always had a roving eye toward the University of Texas, but it would be too close to home. I could just imagine hopping on a bus home after a Saturday morning chemistry quiz to sell clothes to transient workers in our Outlet Store. Our friends, Bully and Josie Gilstrap, kept inviting me to come to Austin and live with them. Bully was a UT football coach on Dana X. Bible's staff. I was certainly not enamored with this idea. However, I did decide to switch plans and go to UT. I canceled reservations at Tech.

Dad said that I must live in the Scottish Rite Dorm at UT. Of course it was too late to get a reservation. Georgia and I were planning to be roommates. We were lucky enough to get into Hinkley House, where thirty-one girls would live, sleep and eat. The house was on University Boulevard, right in front of the famous fountain and across the street from Alpha Phi sorority house. The Kappa Sig house faced the fountain from the far end of University Boulevard. It was a fabulous location close to campus.

We checked into our new home early. We had been invited to go through Rush.

Aunt Pink was a master seamstress. I had always loved the beautiful clothes she made for me. I was probably the best dressed girl in Rosebud, Texas. Few people bought ready-made clothes. Most ladies sewed, and our stores had fabulous fabric departments. Aunt Pink, Mother and I began to plan my college wardrobe. I had worn stitched-down pleated skirts all my life, so this is where we began.

Luscious sweaters and silk blouses would work everywhere. I had a blue plaid full-circle chambray skirt and a solid blue Gibson Girl blouse to wear with black-and-white saddle oxfords and white socks. The rich, dark, chocolate-brown two-piece suit in lustrous cotton poplin had a pleated peplum and tiny gold buttons.

There was a black satin sleeveless cocktail dress with a bustle in the back and a dark-green silk dinner dress featuring a jewel neck, long fitted sleeves and a side-draped skirt. I had shiny black pumps and crystal jewelry to wear with the black dress. Green alligator sling pumps and matching hose were perfect together. I needed a hat for the President's Tea. Pop sent me to an exclusive specialty shop to make the selection. I chose an off-white brushed-wool cloche hat with a gold braided band. I had exquisite gold earrings, a necklace and a bracelet to complete this ensemble. No doubt about it, along with existing wardrobe pieces, I was all set. I did go out and purchase a fuchsia-and-hot-pink moiré taffeta ballerina dress and silver ballet shoes for a special event.

I decided to take a cooking course in the hotel management school across campus. I wanted to learn to make good breads, rolls and cakes, plus frozen desserts. I was required to wear a white uniform and hairnet to class. I thought this would be fun. We had a few "holier than thou" girls in our house that let me know that wearing this outfit was degrading. So, as I walked across campus in my kitchen outfit, I tried to notice folks' reaction. There was none, so I was convinced that everyone was not humiliated by a white uniform and hairnet. I had been taught that honest jobs were honorable and that we should be respectful of others. I still use the recipes that I learned to make so many years ago, but I miss the white uniform and hairnet.

We had lots of fun at UT. We worked all week at putting together the perfect looks for the football game. We danced at Dessau Hall, studied hard, had fun parties and met wonderful people. This was an experience everyone should have.

Georgia and I didn't hang around long enough to get a degree. She married C.L. Kirkley, and they had three daughters and a son. The girls would sometimes join us for RHS Golden Years Reunion in Rosebud. C.L. passed away at an early age. Georgia, the smart girl who was exempt from freshman English at UT, was plagued with ill health for a few years before she passed away one cold day in November 2007. I loved being with daughters Nancy, Linda and Sandra when they brought their mother to Rosebud. Bob and I attended graveside services for our friend, Georgia, in pouring rain. It hurt to give her up, but I am grateful for our years of friendship.

My friends Jimmy Lamar and Robert Summers were students at UT while I was there. We would sometimes meet and sit on the steps at the fountain. They were like big brothers to me. I met them after a chemistry quiz one Saturday. Our quiz was held in an old army barracks, having been added to accommodate the overflow of students. There were open cracks in the floor, and cold air would whistle up into the room. I happened to have Joe Thrasher's RHS football letter sweater, which was heavy and very warm. I decided to wear it this day. Robert told me I should not wear a high school letter jacket or sweater on campus. There were students who would take this item and literally cut off the letter. He said, "Betty Ann, you are no longer in RHS. You are a college student. Don't confuse the two." I was grateful for the information and so glad that I had not been attacked. Live and learn, as the saying goes.

Bully and Josie were sweet to me and always checked to see if all was well. Many years later, I met Bobby Dillon, Ed Heap and Keifer Marshall in Temple, Texas. They all had known Bully as their coach at UT. When Josie passed away, these gentlemen came to Rosebud for her funeral. We all sat together. At the cemetery, Bully held my hand and said, "Betty Ann, we got a good crowd for our sweet Josie today, didn't we?"

Textile class at UT was a surprise to me. I could not believe how well-versed I was on fabric content. Architecture was a foreign subject as far as I was concerned. I was never meant to become an artist. This is when I decided that the clothing business was exactly where I needed to be.

THE GILDA FORMAL

Rita Hayworth's famous black strapless evening dress in the movie *Gilda* caught my eye. I just had to have this exotic formal gown to wear to Round Up at UT. My uncle G.B. was with Slater-White Laundry in San Antonio. They covered their steam presses in the best black taffeta that money could buy. He sent me several yards of this fine fabric. Aunt Pink designed and made the dress. My mother had something to say about the finished product—it would have shoulder straps two inches wide. There would be three huge silk roses in pink cascading down one side, and the glamourous matching jacket with full crushed sleeves would be lined in pink satin.

My date was Charles Dowis from Marlin, who was a UT student. He asked my friend, Jeanie, who was in nurse training at Seaton Hospital, what my favorite flower would be. She said, "Dyed blue gardenias." This was supposed to be a joke, but that is exactly what arrived at the house the afternoon of the big party. So the blue gardenias were substituted for the pink roses! I wasn't even excited about doing away with the straps. And the jacket with the lush pink lining was lost! My glamourous Rita Hayworth ensemble was a huge disappointment! But—one did not dare to insult a date by not wearing his flowers! The pink roses had to go. Good manners will overrule every time!

OUR WEDDING

Bob and I dated for six months and decided to marry. Plans were made, and the date was set on my little sister's birthday. She was furious! We were taking the spotlight on her day. I can't imagine what I was thinking.

Our beautiful First Methodist Church burned to the ground three days before our wedding. Bob was a volunteer fireman and first to arrive at the fire station after the alarm sounded. He drove the fire truck to the church.

The Thrashers lived across the street from the church, and Bob's bedroom was at the rear of the house. The fire at the church was started on the backside where the Boy Scouts met. So Bob had no idea where the fire was until he arrived at the station.

Aunt Rose was taking Bob and me to Dallas the next morning to select furniture as her wedding gift. We did take the planned trip to Dallas amid very sad feelings. My lifelong plans to marry in my precious church were not going to happen. This was a sad day.

Every church in Rosebud offered to let us have the ceremony in their facility. Bob had grown up in the Baptist church, so we decided to have our wedding there. Reception plans had gone by the wayside, so we opted to have the event at our favorite restaurant, El Tampico. This building was beautiful, with several huge sparkling crystal chandeliers.

Rosebud Roses

Tony and Margaret Bienhauer owned the Bienhauer Bakery three doors down from The Leader. They were giving us our gorgeous wedding cake as their gift. Jackie and Jiggs Walston had the jewelry store and florist. They had been commissioned to create our floral arrangements. Because of all the tragedy, they insisted their floral arrangements be accepted as gifts. We could not believe the generosity and kindnesses that came about that day.

We decided on New Orleans for our honeymoon. Our wedding was at three p.m., and we spent the night in Houston before continuing on to our destination. We had left my coat behind, so we waited for our friends, Betty and Bob Lucas, to bring it to us. They lived in Houston and had attended our wedding.

Mary Jane Sapp was my maid of honor. Billie Jean Vlha was my bridesmaid. Joe Eber Thrasher was Bob's best man. My brother, Thomas Frank Tapman, was groomsman. Thomas Earl Anding and John William Schigut were ushers. John William was also the soloist who sang "Because" and "Always." Mrs. Ruth Nabers was pianist. Reverend Donald Box officiated—he was the Methodist minister and our close friend.

The next morning we began our journey to New Orleans. Wanting a cup of coffee, we detoured, ending up in Eunice, Louisiana. Immediately, we were met with a violent thunder storm and horrendous rain. It was very dark and looked terribly dangerous, so it made sense to settle in for the night. There was only one hotel in this small town. Bob accidentally locked the keys in the car. We registered in the old hotel and were making our way up the creaking staircase when we met a young couple coming down. They said, "If you can stay here, you are better than us." As we entered our antiquated room, I sat on the bed, and it went all the way to the floor. It was horrible, not just less than desired.

When daylight finally arrived, it was still stormy. Bob broke the car window with a tire tool. Now we needed to get the window

Betty Thrasher

replaced, which seemed to take forever. At last, our beautiful, new white Pontiac was in one piece.

Arriving in New Orleans was a welcomed relief. We had a great honeymoon after all!

Bob and Betty's wedding reception was held February 6, 1949, at El Tampico after the church burned. Aunt Pink and Uncle Boss can be seen over Bob's right shoulder.

WACO, TEXAS

On May 11, 1953, a terrible tornado came down on Waco, Texas. Bob had gone to Waco to attend a Pontiac meeting on Franklin Avenue, and I kept watching the dark green sky. I was expecting our second son on July 4. It is a miracle that Michael Tapman Thrasher was not born on this day in May.

The sky became more frightening, and I was very concerned for Bob's safety. Sure enough, this powerful tornado roared into Waco and left a terrible path of deadly destruction. Many lives were lost, and buildings were totally demolished. As the news spread, our fears grew greater and greater. Bob was planning to go to the Joe L. Ward auto paint shop. On the way there, a huge tree fell across the Austin Avenue in his path. This was a warning to be still until the storm settled.

The area of town where Bob was headed had been destroyed! Sirens were blaring, and lights were flashing from every direction. There was an extreme state of emergency! No one was allowed to enter the city of Waco except emergency vehicles from nearby towns. No one was allowed to leave the city, and no calls could be made unless they were emergencies. Waco was almost completely shut down. Doctors, hospitals and emergency crews were overwhelmed. It was late evening before I heard from Bob.

I fully expected my own emergency because of all the anxiety that day, but baby Michael was quite calm and arrived on July 2.

JEWISH FRIENDS

Our family looked forward to Thursday evenings, when we drove to Waco for dinner and a serious visit to the Freeman Kosher Delicatessen. We enjoyed various sandwiches of pastrami, corned beef and a variety of mouth-watering cheeses on their famous Jewish rye bread. I can still taste their Russian dressing and real kosher pickles.

After dinner, the stories were shared about Jewish friends, families and acquaintances who were fortunate to escape the German prison camps during World War II. We knew a few who had somehow escaped from the horror of the death chambers, and one of these friends joined us on Thursday evening events.

Waco was home to many Jewish families. The Goldsteins and Migels had a department store. I did not have the pleasure of knowing these gentlemen, but I admired Monte Lawrence for his beautiful posture and big smile. He and the Freeds, Ann and husband Abby, were important figures in the Goldstein-Migel store. The Freds were jewelers. The Sachs brothers worked with their father on Austin Avenue, and later, both Jack and Aubrey had their own clothing stores for ladies. Nate Chadrow's upholstery fabrics were luxurious, and I could spend hours at his store. My friend, Mildred Skelton, bought some silk brocade fabric there and made a sophisticated cocktail outfit and trimmed it in mink fur.

When I was a young child, we would visit the Fleisher family in Cameron, Texas. Abe was a well-rounded businessman. His wife, Sue, was an attractive brunette with a happy smile, and I remember her delicious spritz cookies

Mrs. Siegal owned a grocery store in Eddy, Texas, and was a frequent visitor to the Cruvand home in Rosebud. She gave me a real diamond ring when I was in middle school. My little brother asked to see the ring. He threw it into Aunt Rose's front yard. We searched and searched but never found the ring.

When I had children of my own, we drove to San Antonio to visit Uncle Sol's nieces. Their husbands, Harrell Franzel and Paul Pearlstone, had a children's clothing manufacturing business, The Texan, that featured quality clothes for small children. I recall buying a grey gambler-stripe western suit for Bobby when he was three years old. We found a great pair of mustard-colored Acme western boots for him. This was photographed, and I thought it was one of his cutest outfits. I still love this picture. Goldie Pearlstone was quite a sophisticated socialite who loved to entertain. Ginnie Franzel was a good swimmer and a talented golfer. It was at the Franzel home that I learned to love my matzo pancakes with red plum jelly. This is still a favorite!

We all loved to see Harvey and Lois Zidel at The RoseBud. He entertained us while Lois shopped. Gloria Brickman would bring friends to our store quite often. Yvonne and Arnold Miller were fun to see. We loved hearing about his summer camp for children from Israel. Simone Bauer loved exciting clothes, and Rose Jacobson was an elegant lady.

Lorraine Hoppenstein was a regular customer whose impeccable taste leaned toward smart, tailored fashion in good fabric. Her husband, David, was big into real estate. We loved his stories.

The RoseBud presented several Hadassah fundraiser shows at the Brazos Club. We met some fabulous Jewish people at these events. I was excited to meet Mrs. Wolfe, of Wolfe Flowers.

Rabbi Wolfe Macht was a very special friend of our family. He visited our stores on a regular basis, and he officiated at my uncle Sol Cruvand's funeral. He tried to convince me to attend Baylor University.

The Snayman family hosted luncheons for Uncle Sol's and Aunt Rose's funerals. When my dad's obituary appeared in the Waco papers, several Jewish friends called to offer their condolences and help. This was so important to me.

Evelyn Hoffman and Jean Adelman taught me so much about Jewish history. Jean had children living in Israel, and when they came home for a visit, they found time to jaunt over to The RoseBud in Temple for a quick visit!

Evelyn Hoffman devoted the entire thirty minutes of her television show, *Better with Age*, to the models for the annual Scott & White "Holiday Extravaganza" fundraiser every year. This was a great way to get the word out to hundreds of folks! We could have never afforded a better thirty-minute commercial! I was amazed when a group of Coryell County bass fishermen told me they saw this program and loved it! We never know who may be watching!

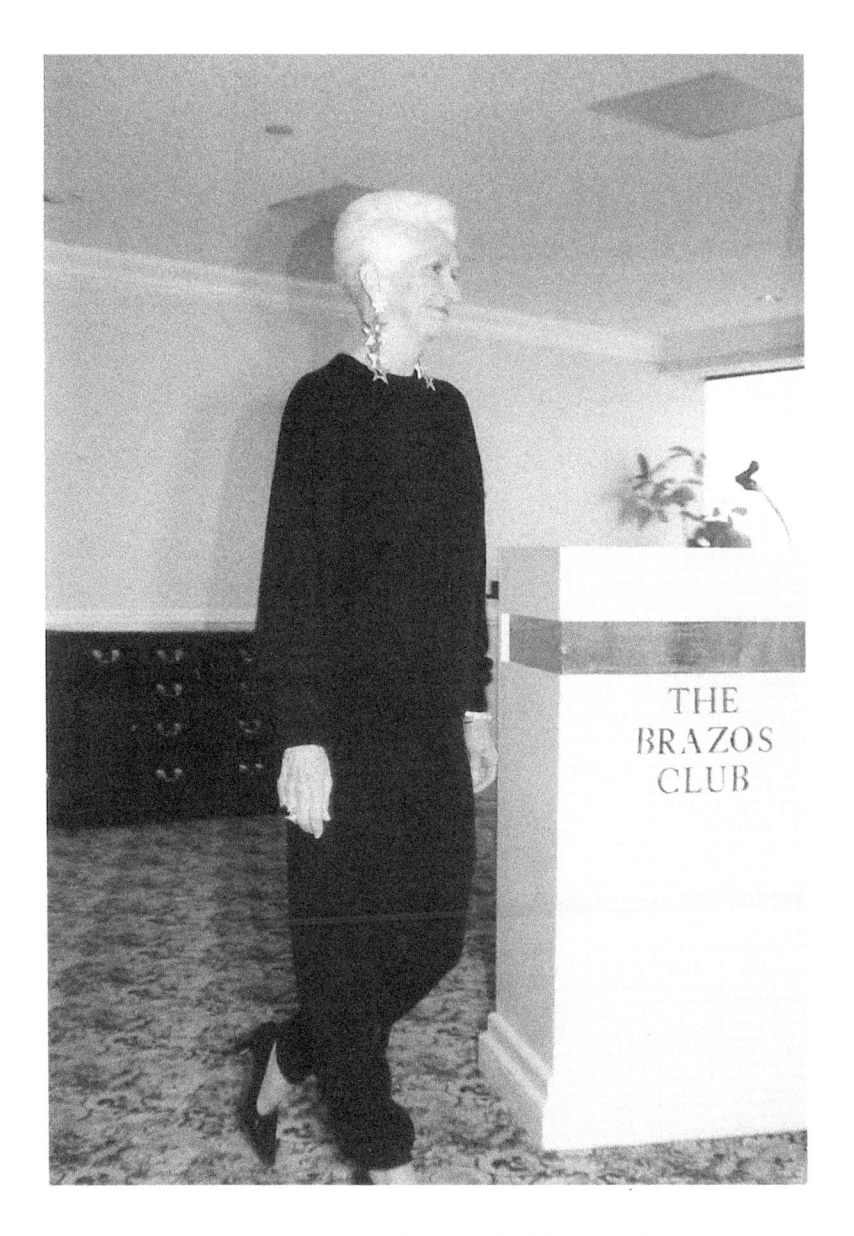

Mary Purifoy sharing fashion with
Hadassah at Brazos Club in Waco.

THE HOLOCAUST

My father's Jewish parents came to America in the middle 1800s from Russia and landed at Ellis Island, New York. They settled in St. Louis, Missouri. After my dad's death in 1988, I had a nagging desire to visit one of the Jewish death camps in his honor. We had friends who survived the Holocaust and lived to tell about the horrors. My family also brought a Jewish refugee to this country.

My friend, Dr. Barbara Amaral, was an oncology specialist at Scott & White Hospital in Temple, Texas. She was a tall, lean, attractive woman who loved to dress up for her patients. She believed that her appearance had a profound effect on them. Bobbie came to The RoseBud quite often, and it was easy to see how her day materialized. Sometimes, she would just sit quietly and have a cup of coffee. Other times, she would be in the mood to shop for a new outfit. We always allowed her to decide.

She often shared beautiful stories with me, and the one I loved most was about a young man who had terminal cancer. He was handsome and very intelligent. His young wife was beautiful, and the couple was very much in love. When Bobbie came by on her rounds each day, he would say, "I can hardly wait to see what you will be wearing today." After he passed away, the young wife thanked Bobbie for looking beautiful on her visits and was grateful that she didn't always walk into his room in a white lab coat. Bobbie was a positive sight for this young man, whose life and happiness were cut so short.

Dr. Amaral had practiced medicine in Munich, Germany, for five years while her husband, Dr. Bill Amaral, was in the US Army. Bobbie modeled for The RoseBud and was a crowd favorite on our runways.

Through our many conversations, I must have expressed a desire to visit one of those awful concentration camps. She suggested that she and I plan a trip to Europe and dash through seven countries in three weeks, just hitting the high spots along the way. Since Bobbie had a keen knowledge of where to travel, she planned our itinerary. High on the list was Dachau, Germany.

When we entered this prison camp, it was absolutely impossible to understand how Hitler managed to bring such slaughter to the Jews. I could hardly imagine how many great minds were destroyed at the hands of Hitler. What a tragedy. Just thinking about all these men, women and children made me tremble, and I felt hot tears roll down my cheeks. I was overcome with grief.

How could this civilized world allow such a thing to happen? I could hardly compose myself. Oh, how I wished I could have had my dad and Uncle Sol with me as I stumbled away from the Dachau Camp. I needed their strength, and at the same time, I knew this would have broken their hearts. However, maybe it was a tribute to those who sacrificed so much that we had made such an effort to feel their pain. We will always grieve for those who suffered so terribly during this ordeal.

It is so important that we all remember the Holocaust and never allow this to happen again. In these trying times, we must make ourselves aware of such tragedy and never cease to be aware of those who say that the Holocaust never happened.

Never again!

It still bothers me that, in the early years, Jews were denied membership in the fancy, big-time private clubs! It made no difference if they held high degrees in education! However, it seems that we all know about the fabulous contributions made by Jonas Salk, Albert Einstein, Mark Chagall, Leonard Bernstein and so very many more bright minds! And—just think about the destruction of the Holocaust!

Today, we wear the labels of talented designers such as Ralph Lauren, Calvin Klein, Levi Strauss and many others! We admire Hollywood actresses and actors for their talent in films and on Broadway—such as Elizabeth Taylor, Barbara Streisand, Paul Newman, Harrison Ford, William Shatner, George Gershwin—just to name a few! How about Alan Greenspan, chief lecturer, economist and—pianist!

TV cohost of Joan Rivers' Fashion Police, Leon Hall, pictured with the RoseBud models: Patti Thrasher, Kay Roberts, Linda Ringler, Betty Thrasher, Moni Roming and Georgia Tarver

MY HOMETOWN

As I look back on my life, I know that I am a very wealthy person—not so in dollars and cents, but in family, friends and unforgettable experiences. I will never forget the folks who were such an important part of my life! They had strong faith and great hopes for all the children of Rosebud, Texas. It was just understood that each of us would go out into this big ole world and make tremendous strides and accomplishments—each of us in his own way!

It has been said that parents are not too smart until their children reach the age of forty. What a big surprise! I often think what a tremendous impact my family had on me. How could I not have seen this during my early years? Why did it take so long to realize how many positive gifts they showered on me while I was growing up?

My parents expected us to be respectful, kind and well mannered. Just in case we had a lapse in memory, my beautiful mother had a special "look." She never had to say a word when she gave us that look! This was a pretty clever way of disciplining kids! It took absolutely no stress, strain or physical energy, and no belt, paddle or switch—just love! (This is how she explained it, and we would never dare to contradict this lady!) We all had expectations to live up to, and we certainly understood that we were committed to meet these responsibilities.

So I want to emphasize the fact that the priceless gifts I received all those years long ago came from a special breed of folks I like to call my extended family! It would be impossible to forget the special ones who became a part of my life! I know that they are all looking down from heaven upon all the kids who passed through Rosebud.

Special thanks go to:

1. Uncle Sol Cruvand for his wisdom.
2. Aunt Rose Cruvand for her intellect.
3. Mother for her contagious laugh and concern for others.
4. Dad for his salesmanship and kind heart.
5. Aunt Johnnye for her talents with hairstyling and makeup.
6. My sister, Peggy, for her friendship and compassion.
7. My brother, Bubba, for his sweet smile and way with people who loved this hero 'til the end.
8. My husband, Bob, for his love and support.
9. And to all the people of our town for their faith and trust in me.
10. Aunt Pink for her excellent talent and ability for design.

I am now in the twilight years of this rich life! How did I get here so fast? The memories are overwhelming. Our two incredible sons each gave us a grandson. One grandson gave us two handsome great-grands! My daughter-in-law, Patti, is my best friend. My wonderful parents, aunts, uncles and brother have gone on to a better place, but their presence will always be felt. The best memory is of those who called Rosebud home. What a powerful "growing up" we had!

The age-old story of that little town in Central Texas called Rosebud is forever etched in our minds. A story like this never, ever ends!

PART II
OUR MEN IN THE MILITARY

"Fashion is the armor to survive the reality of everyday life."
—Bill Cunningham

OUR MEN IN THE MILITARY

JAMES CHANCE, WAR OF 1812

James Chance was born on December 30, 1795. He grew up in Montgomery County, Georgia, and Felicianna Parish, Louisiana.

During the War of 1812, James served as a private under Captain Isaac Townsend in the Louisiana Militia. James married Miss Sarah Ann Harrell on June 29, 1818, in Saint Francisville, Louisiana. James and Sarah relocated to the Republic of Texas on November 18, 1840.

James and Sarah passed away in Milam County, Texas. James died May 20, 1863, and Sarah died April 3, 1862. They were reinterred in the Texas State Cemetery in Austin. Their granddaughter, my grandmother, George Elizabeth Long, was born November 25, 1864. On March 18, 2010, Charlene and Tom Tapman visited the Texas State Cemetery and photographed the grave markers.

DAN AND G.B. LITTLE

My mother's brothers, Dan and G.B. Little, were in the Texas National Guard when it was federalized. These two men joined the army and were sent to France. (L.B. had been in the guard but was not accepted into the army because he was underaged.) When the guys became eligible to go to France, Grandmother requested that they be allowed to stay together in order to protect each other. These were strong, healthy, handsome men. I thought G.B. looked like Clark Gable.

As the WWI troop train arrived at the Rosebud Depot after the war, twin sisters Tommie and Johnnye, sisters of Dan and G.B., raised the Stars and Stripes to begin the welcome home ceremony. Their sister, Pink, had designed red, white and blue bunting outfits with matching hats for the twins to wear to this special homecoming ceremony. This must have been a glorious day in Rosebud, Texas.

HARRY M. TAPMAN

My dad was about to enter the service when armistice was signed, so he never served in our armed forces.

ALLAN GRAY LITTLE

My first cousin, Allan Gray Little, moved to San Antonio with his parents, Pauline and G.B. Little, and little brother, Dwight, when he was eleven years old. G.B. became the engineer for Slater-White Laundry, which covered a city block in San Antonio. Very wealthy, well-known folks sent their table linens to Slater-White.

Allan graduated from Thomas Jefferson High School and attended A&M College in College Station, Texas. He decided to join the army as a private. Thirty-eight years later, he retired as a colonel.

Allan was aide to General Omar Bradley, the last of the five-star generals. Allan was with the general the last two and a half years of the general's life. By this time the general was in a wheelchair due to serious arthritis in his knees from playing football at West Point.

I was in Dallas for market when I walked into my hotel room and flipped on the TV. I could not believe my eyes when I saw Allan with General Bradley at President Ronald Reagan's inauguration! General Omar Bradley was the distinguished grand marshal of Reagan's inaugural parade in Washington! I will never forget this scene.

Col. Little worked his way through the ranks and was accepted into officer candidate school. He was commissioned directly from OCS into the Transportation Corps based upon his personal request. He was inducted into the Artillery OCS Hall of Fame in 1986.

Allan and his wife Lisa have both passed away. They were good, God-fearing folks who reared a beautiful family with all children having earned degrees from the University of Texas at Austin. My mother adored Lisa Little.

ROBERT MORRIS (BOB) THRASHER

After graduation from Rosebud High School, Bob Thrasher was hitchhiking to Corpus Christi to find work. He was picked up by the district attorney of Bexar County, Mr. Johnny Shook. He took Bob through the state capitol building in Austin and introduced him to some of his friends. Afterwards, they headed toward San Antonio and ended up at the DA's ranch. During this three-day stay, the DA attempted to talk Bob into going to work for the border patrol. Bob was not impressed with the idea, so they headed to Corpus Christi.

Things were not as rosy as Bob expected, so he decided to join the Thrasher family in Orange, Texas. He got a job as a welder in the Levingston shipyards. The Thrashers returned to Rosebud, and Bob moved in with his good friend, Red Moore. Soon Bob received his greetings from Uncle Sam and was drafted into the army. He served three and half years in the South Pacific as a welder.

Bob was attached to the First Cavalry. He was in New Guinea, Los Negros in the Admiralty Islands, and Leyte, and from there, went to Luzon. (When the war ended he was in Leyte.) This is where General McArthur waded ashore on his return to the Philippines. Bob was discharged at Camp Fannin in Tyler, Texas.

Bob was very ill when he returned from the war. He had

hepatitis and dengue fever. He only weighed one hundred and eleven pounds. And his skin was very yellow. Much rest and good food brought him good health! Years later, Bob had a reoccurrence of hepatitis and was very sick again.

I did not really know Bob until after he was in the service.

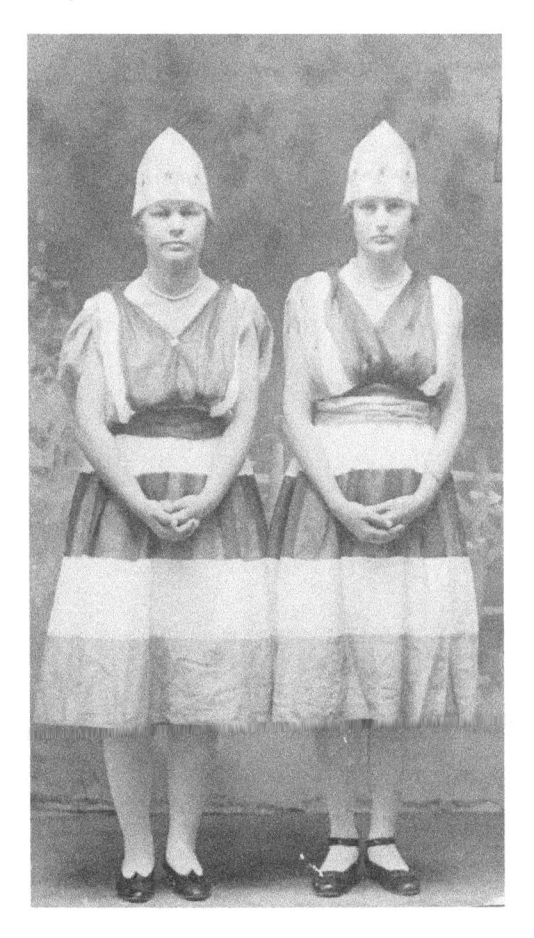

Twin sisters Tommie and Johnnye Little were chosen to raise the flag as the train with WWI troops rode into the Rosebud Depot.

ROBERT MORRIS THRASHER JR.

Robert M. (Bobby) Thrasher Jr. chose Southwest Texas State University in San Marcos, Texas, after graduation from Gatesville High School. Studying was not his number one interest. (He was an avid fisherman.) The Vietnam War was raging, and we were concerned that Bobby would be drafted into the walking infantry, which would most certainly land him into the dangerous jungles of Vietnam. So we suggested that he volunteer for the service of his choice. He joined the United States Air Force and tested in the top 2 percent.

He was to report for induction a few days before Christmas. (This was hard on me.) His first assignment was to Lackland Air Force Base in San Antonio for basic training. On his one official day off, his high school sweetheart, Michelle Wiggins, and I visited him and had lunch at his favorite Mexican restaurant, Mi Tiera, in San Antonio.

The first weekend pass was exciting for all of us. My brother, Major Tom Tapman, USAF, and his family lived in Austin (Bergstrom AFB). Tom and his wife, Charlene, decided to loan Bobby their beautiful Buick Riviera to drive to Gatesville for the weekend. Charlene would pick him up at his barracks. When she drove up, the presence of a beautiful blonde lady in this high-powered swanky car set the whole area on alert! Bobby was escorted to the car, and they sped off—the lowly airman and the major's lady in that grand automobile! Just imagine being sent off in such grand style! (The Tapmans never dreamed that their generous offer would create such attention and excitement. It certainly was rare for this to happen at the basic training facility.)

On another occasion, Uncle Bubba, the major, stopped by the barracks for a short visit. This sent the airmen, along with their sergeant, into orbit! It must have been like a Gomer Pyle movie. (Bobby had lost several inches and looked great.) I guess he just forgot where he was and addressed the major as Uncle Bubba. This was not good!

Bobby was stationed at Keesler Air Force Base in Biloxi, Mississippi, when he learned that his group would be shipping out to London, England. He and Mikie were getting married, and invitations were ready to mail. When Bobby told his commander about his wedding plans, he was told that if the air force had wanted him to have a wife, they would have issued him one! The wedding was moved up, new invitations were printed, and the wedding took place.

Several months later, we sent the bride to London, England, to join her new husband. While on this tour, Jeffery Todd Thrasher was born. It was three months before we were able to hold our first grandson.

After their three years in England, the family came home on leave en route to their new assignment at Homestead Air Force Base in Florida.

COLONEL THOMAS FRANK TAPMAN

From the day he was born on December 3, 1932, he was a joy to his family. He was the most beautiful baby. He had the sweetest smile that he carried with him all through his life. When "Bubba" was born, I was three years old, and I adored him at first sight. I was sure that this darling little baby was my personal gift, like a real live doll! He was a good little boy, and he let me hug him a lot. But there came a time when hugs were off limits.

My brother, Thomas Frank Tapman, was my best friend, and we both knew we could count on each other. He stood for all things good and took his obligations seriously. He loved Rosebud, Texas, and felt so lucky to have grown up in such a special little town. Tom was raised in the First United Methodist Church of Rosebud. He was a Boy Scout and one of Rosebud's fair-haired sons. And he was my little brother!

He had ambition and drive—there was not a lazy bone in his body. Tom Tapman was a great athlete, captain of his football team and president of the R Association. He was a class officer and a friend to his classmates. He loved all sports, especially football, baseball and basketball. He was always a team player.

At an early age, he got a job at Tony Bienhauer's Bakery, baking bread and making doughnuts with his friend Richard Schigut. Tom really did not enjoy working in our stores. He much preferred baling hay or clearing brush for the Rural Electric Company. When one of his supervisors became a new father, Tom, Richard and David (Sapp) were excited to join in the fun by smoking a cigar. It was not nearly so much fun when they all became seriously sick and a little green around the gills. My brother never became a smoker.

Tom chose to attend the University of Texas, where he met two of his closest lifetime friends, Dwain McDonald and Bill Thomson. All of them excelled in their careers. Dr. Dwain McDonald became chief of staff at St. Joseph's Hospital in Fort Worth, married Jane, and they had two children. Bill became a petroleum engineer and was hired as vice CEO of Phillips Petroleum. He and Dot had two daughters, lived in Norway and came home to retire in Houston.

Thomas Frank Tapman was attending UT in Austin when he joined the United States Air Force. Cadet Tapman was stationed in Harlingen when sister Peggy and I decided to visit him. We arrived at the base and tried to locate our brother. We happened upon an airman who knew him. Our new friend told us that Tom was attending a GI party! And then he explained that this meant he was scrubbing barracks floors!

Tom, whom we called Bubba, was dead serious about the air force. He always had a deep desire to be a fighter pilot. After receiving his Navigator wings, he was accepted into pilot training. I drove my parents to Laredo for his graduation. He was dating Charlene Trewitt from Gatesville, and we all met her plane when she flew in for his graduation.

During the graduation ceremony, it was announced that Lt. Tom Tapman was the Distinguished Graduate in the class! Our hearts were about to burst with pride! A magnum of champagne was brought to our table, and we had a huge celebration! It was no surprise to see that he was the man of the hour. He was obviously very popular with all the pilots. It was one of the best times of our lives! We were bursting with pride! We were so proud of Bubba.

The Air Force chooses their best young pilots to attend Top Gun School at Nellis Air Force Base, Las Vegas, Nevada. Again, Tom was the Distinguished Graduate, the best of the best!

Tom rose through the ranks from cadet school to the rank of colonel. He was tops in everything he touched, and it was no accident. He had set his sights on his future as a young man. Being a Top Gun fighter pilot is no small thing. With the honor comes great dangers and responsibility. Colonel Tom Tapman loved his job!

Tom served his country during the Vietnam era and made numerous Pacific crossings in the F-100 aircraft. During his distinguished career, he received many awards and medals. He was a volunteer pilot in the top-secret Misty Fast TACS squadron.

The Mistys are legend! You may read about them in the book *Bury Us Upside Down* by Rick Newman and Don Shepperd. The forward is written by John McCain. Tom's story is on pages 283-287:

> "He was also a favorite of Colonel Schneider. Tapman was an athletic-looking guy and always dressed impeccably—like he had come right off a recruiting poster. He knew his stuff too, and Schneider liked to use him to brief visiting dignitaries. He always came across as knowledgeable and professional."

On April 7, 1968, Major Tom Tapman was scheduled to fly a Misty Mission with Jonesy Jones, who would be making his one-hundredth mission. The plane was shot down on this mission. The pilots ejected and landed in the jungles of Vietnam. Tom had to kill two Vietnamese soldiers before he was rescued. Thanks to God, he was lifted out of that jungle alive! Tom's strong faith and his excellent training, as well as the good common sense he was known to possess, brought him home to us.

This little brother was a special gift, and he was my hero way before he was a Misty. During his distinguished career, he received many awards and medals. Those he prized the most were the Distinguished Flying Cross, the Purple Heart and the Bronze Star. He flew a total of 410 missions. He had 3,500 hours in his beloved F-100 fighter plane and 1,000 hours in the Vaught Aeronautics A-7D. Tom Tapman was an amazingly brave and valuable man among us!

Tom's last assignment was as Air Force Liaison to the III Corps at Fort Hood. He retired from the US Air Force in 1984. The Tapmans have lived in Belton since 1980. Tom was a member of First Christian Church in Belton. He served the church as deacon, elder and trustee for thirty-four years.

Christmas Day 2014 was a happy event. The Bob Thrasher family, Bobby, Jeffery, Cheri, Tristen and Trevor celebrated this special time in the home of Dr. Michael and Patti Thrasher in Waco. The day was joyous, the food was delicious and the gifts were fabulous.

Early the next morning, we received word that Tom Tapman was in critical condition on life support in ICU at Baylor Scott & White Memorial Hospital in Temple, Texas. Our hearts seemed to stand still as we rushed to the hospital. His devoted wife, Charlene, children Tammy and Trey, grandson Chris and wife Anne, sister and brother-in-law Peggy and Jimmy Jobe, Bob and I were standing together all day. Doctors told us that there was no hope for Tom to recover. He passed away late in the evening of Friday, December 26, 2014. Tom's faith was very strong, and we know that he is in heaven with loved ones who have gone on before him.

Colonel Tom Tapman's service was held on Wednesday, December 31, 2014, at Dossman Funeral Home Chapel in Belton with Minister Reverend Michael Dunson officiating. His final

Betty Thrasher

resting place is Central Texas Veterans Cemetery with Military honors, United States Air Force.

Tom was an avid Longhorn until he drew his last breath. He was a highly respected individual and loved by everyone who knew him. He was my little brother, who carried that sweet smile to the end of life on earth and all the way to heaven. I miss him so!

Rest well, little brother "Bubba." You are our Real American Hero!

Colonel Thomas Frank Tapman, Top Gun Fighter Pilot.

THE FLAG

When the 36th Division came to North Fort Hood every year for training, they flew the most enormous United States of America flag that I have ever seen! On our way from Gatesville to Rosebud, I pulled over to the side of the road. I stopped the engine, and my little boys, Bobby and Mike, and I got out of the car! I shared with them the true meaning of this magnificent flag as we stood there in amazement! This profound feeling came over me as I realized their reaction to this beautiful flag! I explained that this flag was a guarantee of freedom for all citizens of our great country! I could not even imagine what it would be like to live in a land filled with fear and heartache! We take so much for granted!

PART III
GATESVILLE

"Fashion is not something that exists in dresses only. Fashion is in the sky, in the street. Fashion has to do with the ideas, the way we live, what is happening."

—Coco Chanel

MOVING TO GATESVILLE

In 1952, the three Thrashers—Bob, Betty and baby Bobby—made the big move to Gatesville, Texas. This was a big step. Rosebud had been home for all our lives, and we had family there. Of course, we knew everyone in town.

After returning from the service, Bob joined his dad in the Bert Thrasher Pontiac Dealership. When Pennington Pontiac in Gatesville went on the market, Bob purchased this business. In one way, we were excited about this venture, but on the other hand, we were sad to leave Rosebud.

The army's summer Longhorn Maneuvers at Fort Hood were well underway, and the town of Gatesville was booming. There were no houses to buy or rent, so Bob commuted from Rosebud to Gatesville for a while. We were very lucky when Miss Vera, who lived alone in her big, beautiful two-story home on Main Street, offered to let us live in the downstairs area while she moved upstairs. This was the perfect solution for all concerned. We took her up on her offer and packed up for the move to Gatesville.

In the afternoons, Bobby and I would sit in the big porch swing and watch the cars parade up and down Main Street. Before baby Bobby was three, he could identify every vehicle on the road by name! We have always wondered just how this little boy could do this when he could not read. Or could he?

When Bob began his daily commute to Gatesville, Mayor Roger Miller, a prominent businessman, invited him to his home for lunch. Bob could not have met a nicer man. Bob made friends quickly and became active in the community. No one came to call on me, so Bobby and I continued to watch the cars go by and wondered when someone would stop and welcome us to town. We finally told Bob that if someone didn't knock on our door soon, Bobby and I would just go back to Rosebud where people were friendly and welcomed newcomers with open arms.

Bob recognized Cub Poston at Lions Club. Cub had lived in Rosebud when he was growing up, and Bob remembered his "dancing eyes." His family owned the International Harvester dealership. Soon, Yvonne Poston came to see me and said that she would be hosting a six-table bridge luncheon in my honor. I was thrilled and excited to meet the Gatesville ladies.

During the course of the lovely party, my bridge partner, a cute little blonde, evidently did not appreciate my bid and proceeded to throw her cards up in the air! I was shocked but managed to maintain my calm. I pushed back my chair, stood and thanked my hostess for such a lovely party and the opportunity to meet such wonderful ladies. I told them that the game of bridge was not my claim to fame, but that I was excited to make the city of Gatesville my home for many years to come and that I would appreciate the opportunity to get to know each of them better. From then on, I had more invitations to bridge parties than I felt I could accept.

I did develop a friendship with the Chrysler dealer's wife and attended a bridge party in their home. I relied heavily on my college wardrobe and wore my forest-green bouclé knit dress that day. I popped a big, red silk rose on my shoulder. My hostess, Tribble Shepherd, said, "Betty, no one but you would have the guts to wear that!"

Several ladies commented on the red rose, so I explained how

Rosebud Roses

much I loved accessories. I took the rose and passed it around, asking the ladies to try it on and give an opinion as to how it made them feel. I explained that I grew up in a clothing store, and at an early age, my mother taught me how to use accessories to an advantage. The ice was finally broken.

Bob was in a group of men that played in pro-am golf tournaments on Mondays. These men were from all walks of life. There were lawyers, doctors, news editors, store owners and even a district judge. These tournaments were fun, and on occasion, wives would attend. I was able to cultivate a few more good friends. Gatesville was, for the most part, a close community and not well known for accepting newcomers who could not claim bones in the cemeteries. But I guess we became the exception to the rule. Bob was handsome, friendly, athletic, played competitive golf and was a great dancer. It just took a while for these folks to warm up to me.

Soon, ladies were dropping their kids off at school and coming by our house for coffee and conversation. I tried my hand at golf, but this was not my game. I was better at hairstyling, skin care, makeup, gift wrapping, cooking and fashion. So, in time, I was able to carve out my niche in Gatesville. The rest is history.

THE FIRST GATESVILLE HOUSE

When we decided to buy a house in Gatesville, there was only one new house for sale on Oak Drive, a nice neighborhood close to the schools. We soon discovered that there was a certain ritual one had to contend with.

Ollie Little's Home Lumber Company builds the house. George Painter's Real Estate sells the house. Gatesville Savings and Loan finances the house, and Horace Jackson Insurance Company insures the house: no exceptions to the rule. I was only twenty-one years old, but I had been blessed with some pretty good teachers.

Before closing the deal, I requested that the backyard be closed in with white picket fencing because we had a small child. The house was pale green with yellow shutters. I wanted the shutters white, so they would need to be painted. The gentlemen agreed to my requests at no additional cost. I waited for weeks for the work to be done. They painted the shutters, but the fence did not materialize. I borrowed a pickup from Bob Thrasher Pontiac, drove it next door to Home Lumber Company and had the fencing loaded in the truck. It was not long until the backyard was childproof and Bobby could safely play outside.

All these men were on the board of Gatesville Savings and Loan Company, and they became our friends. When my store materialized years later, their families were my customers.

THE GATESVILLE COUNTRY CLUB

We were charter members of the Gatesville Country Club. This was the first time I had ever seen or heard of sand greens. I shall never forget the first organizational meeting in the city auditorium.

Plans were being finalized for the club, and there was some controversy in the various opinions of the members. Francis Caruth, a prominent businessman, stood up and said, "What are we building—a church house or a country club?" Gatesville came out of this discussion with a thriving organization and many good folks as members. This was a pretty town, graced with some really beautiful homes and thriving businesses.

Our little family thoroughly enjoyed this facility. Bob and the boys were good golfers, but the sport was not for me. I made myself available to help plan and decorate for social events. The boys and I would spend days there in the summers. I read books while they golfed and swam.

THE TRANSPORTER

Gatesville was a dry town—not a liquor store in sight. Rosebud was a wet town with at least two liquor stores, and for as long as could be remembered, this place had been wide open. When we visited our friends in Rosebud, we were offered coffee or tea. In Gatesville, it was a different story—one was offered beer, wine or something stronger. So it was no surprise when friends and acquaintances began asking me to bring various supplies from the liquor store. Actually, I thought nothing was strange about these requests. My dad would accompany me to C.A.'s Liquor Store. We would load the bottles in the trunk. Sometimes, I would have a pretty big load. We would take our places in the car, with baby Mike in the backseat and little Bob in the front passenger seat. It would not be long before both boys were in a deep sleep and we were cruising down the highway to our home in Gatesville.

One day, Bob looked at me and said, "Betty, do you know that you could get in serious trouble for bringing liquor into a dry territory?" Well, no, I did not know this, so had never thought about such a thing. Suddenly, I could just see the headlines in the newspapers: "Mother with Innocent Children Caught Bootlegging." It scared me so badly that my operation came to a screeching halt. C.A. lost a very good regular customer. Oh well. Ignorance is bliss. I am a very law-abiding person.

GATESVILLE CHAMBER OF COMMERCE

One of our local grocers, Pat Hollingsworth, was president of the Gatesville Chamber of Commerce. He approached me to consider coming to work at the chamber. Retired Army Colonel Al Hopkins was the manager. He was a brilliant man who ran a tight ship. I learned a lot from him and took great pride in the office and my job. I even went down to the office on Saturdays and waxed the floor.

We were planning a big political rally, and it became my responsibility to take young Senator Lyndon Johnson to lunch at Mrs. Melton's boarding house. The food was delicious as always, and the senator was impressed.

The next time I saw this senator, he was running for the office of Vice President of the United States of America! I adored John F. Kennedy, so I became quite interested in the campaign. I personally met Jackie and the Kennedy sisters at a coffee in Waco, Texas. This was even more exciting because I had grown up in an active Democratic environment in Rosebud.

LEAIRD'S

Byron Leaird was a prominent member of the Gatesville Chamber of Commerce. He called me one day and asked me to go to market with him and his wife, Grace, the next day. I could feel the desperation in his voice and felt sure he needed help. Leaird's Department Store was one of major importance to Coryell County and the surrounding areas. Mr. Leaird knew that I had grown up in the small-town department store environment. Bob encouraged me to come to Mr. Leaird's aid. We left the next morning for Dallas market at five a.m. I was now officially the Leaird's ready-to-wear buyer. I would receive a 20 percent discount on personal purchases. This was not acceptable to me, so I would write personal orders at market in the name of The Leader in Rosebud in order to purchase these items at wholesale cost. I had never bought clothing at retail. (My family was really not enamored with my working with another store.)

I continued to work with the Leaird family for several years. The first time I had the store employees celebrate Mr. Leaird's birthday, he cried! No one had ever done this for him before. I had Mrs. Melton make a delicious white cake with his favorite flower, blue morning glories, on top.

Mr. and Mrs. Leaird flew to Detroit to pick up a new car to drive home. While they were gone, I had Bob go into the woods, cut tree branches and spray them white. I had everyone making apple blossoms with pink tissue paper. When the Leairds arrived at the store in their new car, all the outside windows were decorated with apple blossom trees and fabulous fashions. This theme continued inside the store. They were absolutely speechless! We were all so excited to share in the spirit.

The three of us (Byron, Grace and I) were at market when we stopped by a liquor store on Commerce Street in Dallas. I bought Bob some bourbon. Mr. Leaird insisted on taking it to his room and said he would give it to me when we returned to Gatesville. I guess he thought I would drink it. I had to laugh to myself.

On another market trip, I convinced Mr. Leaird to buy three mannequins. As we left market, we put Grace on a plane to New Mexico, and we picked up the disassembled mannequins and placed them in the back seat of the car. Heads, hands and legs were coming from all directions. We stopped for gas, and as the attendant was putting gas in the car, he saw the body parts in the back seat and ran away screaming.

The next morning, we put the beautiful new mannequins together and dressed them "fit to kill." Mr. Leaird's mother, a very refined lady, came to the store to see our prized purchases. She took one quick look, covered her face and said, "They look just like son's cows!" So much for positive excitement. However, the mannequins became very important fixtures. We sold lots of wonderful women's fashions at Leaird's Department Store.

TEE PEE CAFE

Bob was playing in a golf tournament when he became very ill. He was preparing to enter into an exciting new business. In the meantime, a friend needed someone to manage his cafe until he found full-time help. Bob liked the business and enjoyed the customers. His doctor called me at Leaird's and said, "Betty, Bob is very sick." The hepatitis he came down with while serving in the South Pacific had returned. Since Bob had leased the business, I had no choice but to leave Leaird's and run the Tee Pee Cafe.

I had never been behind the counter of a cafe, but I knew how to work! The cafe opened at five thirty a.m. and closed at eleven p.m. We had great cooks. Each night after closing, the furniture was stacked so the tile floor could be wet-mopped. There was quite a procedure to follow each evening. The Tee Pee was sparkling clean when it came time to open for business. Our employees were very loyal until I asked the dishwasher to turn up the heat on the water. Without a word, she took off her apron and said, "I quit!" Thank goodness I knew how to wash dishes, mop floors and even prepare meals.

Bob was prescribed complete rest for several weeks, and our two little boys stayed with our neighbors who always babysat them. Everyone was in place, and the cafe ran like a top. One evening, five generals came for dinner. They liked the food so much they returned again and again while visiting North Fort Hood in Gatesville.

Bob regained his health and took over the cafe, and I resumed life as a stay-at-home mom.

FERN AND GAINES SAUNDERS

We were living in Gatesville with our two small sons when I was asked to come to work at the Chamber of Commerce. My neighbor, Fern, suggested that I take the job and hire her to take care of our boys. This was a perfect solution.

Fern had polio when she was a child and was left a little crippled. One of her legs was shorter than the other, and because of this, she walked with a limp. Gaines was a tall, grandfatherly man who worked at Fort Hood. He adored the boys, Bobby and Mike. On Saturdays, Gaines loved to take them to Greenbriar Creek and the Auction Barn. The Saunders had no children of their own, so they were like grandparents to our boys. They even took them on trips to North Carolina to visit Fern's family.

One day Gaines became ill, and Dr. Wendell Lowrey, who was a fabulous diagnostician, discovered that he had an aneurism in the aorta. He made arrangements for Gaines to see Dr. Michael DeBakey in Houston in order to have the necessary surgery at Methodist Hospital. There was just one problem. Who would drive them to Houston? Fern did not drive, and, for sure, Gaines could not risk driving. Bob and I decided that I would be the designated driver. We would be in Houston about two weeks after the surgery.

We were all poor as church mice and had no idea where we

could afford to stay. I decided to search the motels on South Main Street for the best bargain. One owner took pity on us and offered us a one-room situation for ten dollars per day. Most folks flew into Houston, so it was rare for us to have a car. We were concerned about some other folks, so we offered to transport them to and from the hospital. All of us had patients in ICU and could only visit at certain times, so we spent many hours just sitting in a waiting room between visits. We all became very close and concerned about each other's patients.

There was a handsome high school boy who broke his neck in a football game. His parents had divorced, and each had remarried. These four people were so very kind and considerate of each other! Their first and foremost concern was that precious young man in ICU! We got to know these people well and would stop by their son's bed during our visits. When he was able to be moved into a private hospital room, we visited him. He would always ask about my boys, so when Bob brought them to see us one weekend, we took them to visit our football star. They were delighted to meet each other! Fern and I were able to wish our friends good luck the day their patient was released from the hospital!

We had become close to another friend while in Houston. He was from Georgia, and his wife was very sick in ICU. We thought he was a very poor man, so we tried to take care of him. He asked us to have dinner with him one night. And, lo and behold, he took us to the elaborate and very famous Shamrock Hotel.

I guess that by now it is obvious that we were not able to go home in two weeks. When Gaines came out of surgery, he was paralyzed from the waist down. It was three months before he could be moved into a private room. When someone would come to Houston for a weekend, I would get to go home. On one such weekend, we learned that Uncle Morris Swartz had passed away. My family decided that I would be the one to take Aunt Dora to

St. Louis. Just two weeks before, it was decided to move Gaines into a private room at St. Luke's Hospital. Fern would be able to stay in the room with him. This was a blessing for all concerned. Fern and Gaines would be together, and I could finally go home to my family.

I proceeded to take Aunt Dora to St. Louis. We flew out of the Waco airport to Dallas and changed planes to St. Louis. This was quite an experience! This was an orthodox Jewish service, and we were staying in a kosher home. I was mortified because I had had no exposure to these customs and rituals. However, Clara, our hostess, was wonderful as she guided me through.

After the funeral, we arrived at the airport in Waco. Bob and the boys were nowhere in sight. Three of my closest friends, Billie Jean, Corrine and Mildred were there. Mildred met me as I came off the plane and had me take a pill. (I thought this was because I was exhausted. Wrong!) She told me that Gaines had passed away and that Bob and the boys were in Houston with Fern! I literally sank to my knees!

When Gaines died, Fern planned to have him buried in her family plot in North Carolina. Of course, it was out of the question for our family to attend. Gaines' body was taken to Scott's Funeral Home. Fern wanted our little boys with her while making the decisions for the service in Gatesville. The Saunders were devout members of the First United Methodist Church, so the service must be there. Immediately after, we took Fern to the airport in Dallas for the flight to North Carolina. The funeral home transported Gaines. This was a very sad day.

THE INVENTORS

Five brilliant business men got together in Gatesville, Texas. Price Neeley was the numbers man. Don Jake Saunders was the elite artist. Dr. Tom Williams was a dentist. The two brothers, Drs. O.W. and Ellsworth Lowrey, were the brains. O.W., or Wendell, was a fantastic diagnostician, while Ellsworth possessed an inventing mind along with a great personality. He really loved to make furniture and spent many hours in his workshop. All five men were extremely talented.

They put together a remarkable plan and created Medical Plastics Lab. This was the only company of its kind in the world. They bought and manufactured skeletons. The purpose was for doctors, lawyers and medical schools to have real life models in their classrooms, courts and offices for detailed explanations to patients, students and juries.

This was a fascinating business that was highly respected and well-known around the world.

Employees were intensely trained to perform each job in this unique business. Skeletons who possessed the veins and arteries in colors red, blue and green were referred to as Liberace. (They were considered to be in full dress.) Others were called Plain Jane.

My son, Michael Tapman Thrasher, was in Baylor Dental

School in Dallas when Medical Plastics came out with the full-dressed skull that even had a hinged jaw. My mother wanted to give one of these fancy skulls to Michael for Christmas. When we told him about this, he said, "I can't wait! I want it now! The guys at the dental school would go nuts over this." So I pleaded with manager Charlie Wise, and Michael got one of the original models!

There was no stopping point with these original, remarkable men; they went on to create all sorts of body parts and working mannequins. One could find these instruments in every medical center. I was with my mother in a Waco doctor's office when I noticed the spinal column on his desk. It was fun to tell him how this important visual aid came to be.

At our own Scott & White Hospital in Temple, I took every opportunity to ask if they knew about the Lowrey doctors from Gatesville. Those that had no idea who these famous men were got a little story from me.

The Lowreys were personal friends of ours. Wendell and Nell's daughter, Sara, and Ellsworth and Aline's daughter, Katherine, were classmates of our son, Bobby.

Dr. E. decorated a jeep in the school colors, black and gold, and it was enjoyed by many kids at Gatesville High School. Katherine let Michael drive the jeep around town after she went to college.

The Lowreys also founded the Deck Boat Company. Bobby and Katherine bleached their already blond hair to be filmed waterskiing in a Deck Boat commercial.

Ellsworth, Aline, Katherine, Bobby, Michael, Bob and I spent many weekends on Belton Lake for everyone's kids to enjoy the Deck Boat. Sometimes we camped out overnight. Michael had a little plastic fishing boat that he and Dr. E. would get into and change out different propellers on the big boat. Dr. E. was always looking for a better way.

Rosebud Roses

And then Dr. E. had a trailer company named for his two daughters, Katherine and Lynn. The name of this business was Kay Lynn. This invention really took off. These goose-neck trailers could be seen everywhere! And, of course, they were perfect for loading and pulling the famous Deck Boat!

THE MISS TEXAS PAGEANT

I was sitting in the audience enjoying the Miss Coryell County Pageant. The winner would compete in the Miss Texas Pageant in Fort Worth. This was a Miss America preliminary pageant. Heidi Beth Skelton was a contestant and the daughter of our close friends, Mildred and Joe Skelton. As Heidi was being crowned Miss Coryell County, the announcement was made that Betty Thrasher would be accompanying Heidi to the Miss Texas Pageant as her advisor and chaperone. This was shocking news to me! However, I did accept the honor and blindly began getting Heidi prepared for the event.

Heidi was absolutely gorgeous! We had to come up with a talent. Since she was a majorette in the GHS band, we decided on a twirling routine. We worked diligently perfecting the talent, firming the body and practicing proper etiquette and social graces.

The official wardrobe was extremely important. Luckily, my parents had a clothing store in Rosebud, and we could go to the fashion market in Dallas and purchase all the special outfits we needed. We also would need some monetary assistance because this competition could be expensive! My dad gave us two of the most expensive outfits—a lovely white silk Nardis dinner dress and a fabulous hot-pink silk luncheon suit with all the accessories—hat, gloves, shoes and jewelry. We would need a full-time hairstylist to create that all-American hairstyle. We found the perfect one in Fort Worth, and Pop footed the bill!

Our hometown manager was Mike Trewitt. Bob Thrasher provided a beautiful new automobile, and we acquired a laminated sign: "Heidi Beth Skelton, Miss Coryell County." We loaded a small U-Haul trailer with our belongings and headed to Miss Texas Headquarters in Fort Worth!

Our young son, Michael, hopped on his bike and made the rounds in Gatesville, passing out notecards for folks to send to Heidi encouraging her to win. We think she received the most mail that week! Bob and our boys joined Heidi's parents to attend the final night of competition and the crowning of Miss Texas.

Heidi did not place in the top ten, but she made a good showing, and I got a first-class education that week as to what was needed to produce a Miss America!

For ten years, I was a chaperone for Miss Gatesville. As a preliminary to Miss America, this was big business. Our local pageant was among the best in the state. We had the support of the medical and judicial groups as well as parents and private citizens. We opened our pageant to Central Texas College, Temple College, the University of Mary Hardin-Baylor and Baylor University. I visited each of these schools to audition talents. Trained talent was a top priority in order to compete successfully. All of my girls were special, but not all of them were strong competitors in the field of talent. During these ten years, I was fortunate to have three potential winners…and one who deserved to earn the title of Miss America!

Regina Balch was a natural beauty and a serious dancer. She had been an officer in the world-famous Kilgore Rangerettes. She was easy and comfortable to work with, and her mother was great! Gina was so outstanding at Miss Texas that she was invited back the next year as a special dancer.

Betty Thrasher

Sue Yows ran track at Southwest Texas State University in San Marcos. She could come off that track and, in no time at all, emerge as a beautiful all-American girl, with the attitude to match. She was a joy to be with, and her mother was willing to let me be in charge. (This was not always so easy.) Sue told us she could not sing, so we chose singing as her talent! Our very capable and talented manager was J. Don Duncan, and he designed Sue's talent competition. She would sing Nancy Sinatra's "These Boots are Made for Walking."

Our son, Bobby, had a rock-and-roll band, the Rebellions, and they signed on to help Sue with her talent. We purchased antique gold hopsack jeans and black button-down shirts for the boys in the band—Ernest Ochoa, Bob West, Tom Easley, Jim Hix, David Allen and Bobby Thrasher. They looked sharp! Sue wore a black tee, a short gold hip-hugger skirt and good-looking black boots! She was a knockout!

Mr. Hubert Foster, a prominent supporter of the arts in Fort Worth, had attended our local pageant and liked Sue's talent and the Rebellions, so he invited them to perform at the Fort Worth Club one night during dinner. They were a tremendous hit!

We had a pretty good crowd of local supporters the night Sue performed her song. Earlier in the afternoon, Sue had become very sick. We called the doctor, and he paid us a visit. Sue was not getting better, and we were very worried as we prepared to leave the hotel for the auditorium. (The doctor offered to come to the auditorium and check on her, and of course, we took him up on his offer.) As we were approaching the car, Sue could hardly stand up! Don was making a few changes in the movements in her routine just in case she was able to perform. We were devastated. She was so entertaining and surely deserved to present her act. Sue assured us that she could handle the situation, and we did have the doctor standing by. We kept the predicament to ourselves and didn't talk about it. Don and I said a few serious prayers.

The pageant opened with a bang! It was so rousing! The competitions were outstanding in swimsuit, evening gown and talent. It was time for Miss Gatesville's performance! I was on pins and needles! We had a full orchestra accompanying Sue, under the direction of North Texas' John Giordano! My heart was beating full-speed! Sue stepped out on that stage, looking like a movie star, and sang "These Boots are Made for Walking" like it had never been sung before! The audience clapped and roared their approval! At the close of the pageant, winners in each of the three categories were announced. Sue Yows, Miss Gatesville, was winner of the talent award! She was swept away to the press room for what seemed like hours! But what Don and I would always remember is the standing ovation Sue was honored to receive that night! She was fabulous!

The last year I served the Miss Gatesville Pageant was 1969. We had thirty-five outstanding young ladies as contestants. Our theme was "Up, Up and Away." The art department of Gatesville High School made an awesome hot-air balloon to use as a backdrop. And Betty Lynn Buckley was our emcee. (Later, she became famous on Broadway.)

I asked Ann and Abby Freed at Goldstein-Migel in Waco to give me forty pairs of high-heeled patent leather boots in lime, yellow, orange, red and hot pink. They agreed and added a fabulous white beaded chiffon formal gown to the gift for the winner to wear at Miss Texas! I had a manufacturer make forty "go-go" dresses in the colors of the boots. This outfit was used for the opening scene of the pageant with the girls singing and dancing. It was magnificent!

We had such tremendous trained talent in this show—everything from dancing to opera! The winner was Mary Ann

Long, a senior at Baylor. She was such an outstanding young lady! Mary Ann worked her way through Baylor. She was Baylor Homecoming Queen and graduated with a 4.0 grade average. She drove to Casa Mañana in Fort Worth to perform in various events in the evenings. Virginia Crump, Baylor's dean of women, adored Mary Ann.

The Gatesville owner of Dairy Queen, Dan McNeil, gave us $200 toward a talent competition outfit. Again, my dad gave us clothes and footed the hairstyling bill for the week of the pageant. Mary Ann and I made a trip to Lilly Rubin in Dallas for the exquisite red cocktail dress for Mary Ann's routine. We selected the song "For Once in My Life" as her talent. She had a fabulous voice, and we had John Giordano's orchestra accompany her. (The Gatesville medical and law groups backed us.) This girl was amazing!

When the curtain came up on the final night, the overall beauty of the presentation gave us goosebumps! There were some perfect bodies and overwhelming talent in this pageant. When the top ten were announced, Mary Ann's name and title, Miss Gatesville, was called. Don and I could hardly stay in our seats! Then the top five were announced. Again, Miss Gatesville was called! My heart was pounding!

The fourth runner-up was announced.

The third runner-up was announced.

The second runner-up, Phyllis George, was announced. (Phyllis would go on to be crowned Miss America in 1970.)

The first runner-up was next, and I felt like I was hyperventilating! They called Mary Ann's name. The crowd was in shock! Someone made a serious mistake! Everyone was sure that Mary Ann would be our Miss Texas!

The winner played drums for her talent!

At the reception after the pageant, five Miss Americas were in attendance. They were also speechless! What happened? The night of the pageant, Regina was a special dancer. She was heartbroken over the results. Well, the winner definitely was not a Miss America, so Texas' chance at the title was not to be. Something was terribly wrong here.

A meeting of franchise holders was called. Don and I did not go. We felt that our presence would be distracting. (We would only come across as poor losers.) Well, just the opposite was the case. Everyone thought that Mary Ann should have been the winner and that she would place Texas in the finals of Miss America.

There were many dedicated participants in this program. Some of the most prominent franchises resigned that night.

When I met with our people in Gatesville, I laid all the cards on the table and stated that I felt the folks in charge of Miss Texas were not the people we wanted to work with. If the Miss Texas Pageant wasn't legitimate, we should not be part of it. In all good faith, I could no longer support this program. We cancelled our franchise and were very sorry to see this happen. The Miss America Pageant scholarships for women were the largest and most highly respected in the country. I did not feel it was fair for young women to work so hard and not be entitled to an award they had honestly earned.

I had calls from Miss Texas Pageant officials to reconsider my decision to withdraw. The Associated Press contacted me several times for an interview. I declined because I had nothing positive to say. These young women were too precious to me, and I could never guarantee the honesty of the Miss Texas Pageant officials.

Mary Ann is a devout Christian, and this is what she had to say: "Betty, don't be disappointed. God has a better plan for me just around the corner." What a lady!

Mary Ann went on to achieve a higher degree, and she became an airline stewardess, flying fabulous routes. She became the governess for the children of the second in command of the state department in Austria! She reminded me of Maria in *The Sound of Music*. This young lady was a treasure. Don and I were certainly blessed to work with her.

I would miss this marvelous opportunity to work with such special young women, but surely God had something in mind for my future.

MODEL TEEN SCHOOL

After the experience chaperoning Gatesville's first contestant to the Miss Texas Pageant, a preliminary to the Miss America Pageant, I could see the need for intense special training for our local contestants. The Model Teen Program was selected. I asked L.C. McKamie, the Gatesville school superintendent, what he thought about the idea. He liked the program for many reasons and offered the use of the GHS homemaking department after school hours.

The course would last three months, with one meeting each week. The fee was forty-eight dollars. We offered instruction in personal hygiene and grooming, comportment, posture, speech, expression, fashion and overall appearance. The girls and mothers loved it. I was the one instructor, and the students would ask if we could add Saturdays to our schedules. I thought this was a positive effect. On these days, we would bring sack lunches and spend the day creating new hairstyles and makeup techniques. Manicures and pedicures were lots of fun. We had a great time.

Everyone was a winner. Mr. McKamie said that, as he stood in the hallways observing, he could tell which students were involved in the Model Teen School.

From this time on, we were better able to send our beautiful kids out into the world a little better prepared.

During the course, we would model for stores in Lake Air Mall in Waco and stroll through Piccadilly Cafeteria, stopping to talk about the fashions and just strike up conversations with the diners. This experience did wonders to develop self-esteem. The girls would be in charge of selecting the place to have dinner, and we would work on proper table manners. Each week we would take at least four girls. By the end of the three months, the results were amazing, and we were all proud.

At the end of the course, we would have a graduation party and invite parents to see the finished product.

I loved getting to know these students, and we became friends for life.

FORTY YEARS IN BEAUTY COUNSELOR

Paula Weathers recruited me to become a Beauty Counselor. This was a Dart Industries skin care company. I was very impressed with the news that she shared with me. When the company decided to have warehouses, I was selected to have one of them in Gatesville. My primary job would be to train counselors to work with clients in the privacy of their homes. Beauty Counselor was not sold in stores.

Our product was the purest, and our chemist, Maison G. de Navarre, was the best and most highly respected chemist in the business. At age seventy, there was not a wrinkle in his face. Mr. de Navarre was a cosmetic chemist whose four-volume *Chemistry and Manufacture of Cosmetics* has been considered the standard for the cosmetic industry. We all adored him and regarded him as "the father of cosmetic chemistry."

On Monday mornings, my counselors came to me for training. (I also housed product in my warehouse.) Counselors were not required to have product on hand. They took orders and brought them to the meetings each Monday. Orders were processed and available to be picked up the following Monday. Those who lived great distances away could have orders shipped.

Ralph Wilson Sr. lived in Temple, Texas, and was head of

Betty Thrasher

Wilsonart, which was a division of Dart Industries. I already knew Ralph Wilson when I met Justin Dart, who chartered three huge airliners to fly warehouse owners to Hawaii for a weeklong seminar. Our husbands were invited to go along and play while their wives worked. This was a fabulous experience, and we developed long lasting friendships on this trip.

Russell Ricker was on loan to us for five years. (He was president of Tupperware, another division of Dart Industries.) Our area manager, Geraldine Catougno, was a tall, slender redhead from San Antonio. Our group included Grace and Joe Southwell from Oklahoma City, Oklahoma, and Lynn and Bill Frank from Dallas. The six of us became close friends and enjoyed many fun times together. We all came away from Hawaii a lot smarter.

When we boarded our plane in Dallas, the crew was dressed in Hawaiian attire, and we were wined and dined as elegantly as if we were already on the island. Our magnificent hotel was on the windward side of the island, and the view was spectacular. We were sad when the week ended and we boarded our plane for the trip to Dallas.

When we were landing in Dallas, the city was frozen, and we could see no movement on the roads. It was a couple of days before we felt that it was safe to drive home.

Ralph Wilson invited me to his home in Temple to demonstrate Beauty Counselor to the wives of his corporate staff. Everyone in attendance purchased our Right Face Kit, which included three products—cleanser, refresher and moisturizer. We were first interested in sensible skin care. Makeup was secondary but very important. Mrs. Sunny Wilson did not buy our product. When I asked why she was not interested, she said, "Mary Kay Ash is my friend, and I owe my loyalty to her." Later, Sunny and I became friends, and she admitted that she wished she had tried Beauty Counselor.

Beauty Counselor promoted a clean, natural look in makeup. It takes a little longer to carefully master a natural look. Base should closely blend with the color of the skin. Items of color should be clear and natural. Eyes should be emphasized but with soft colors that achieve a natural effect, not like the makeup is painted on or in garish colors. Natural is the key!

In later years our company became known as Vanda Beauty Counselor. Dart decided to sell the company. This was a sad day for our counselors.

And then—a new makeup counter appeared on the scene in major department stores. The containers and product look like Beauty Counselor. We had a tool called Selectra that could determine a skin type and the best colors for a client. This new skin care business has this same tool. I cannot say this for certain, but this new skin care line sure looked like ours. I personally believe that Beauty Counselor would still be with us if Dart Industries had put a bright woman in charge! (I could be mistaken.)

In 1979, I gave up my Beauty Counselor warehouse business and transferred all my counselors to Lynn Frank in Dallas, because I knew she would take good care of my people. They were not just my counselors, they were my friends.

I had dreamed of having an upscale ladies' shop, and since I had celebrated my fiftieth birthday, the time was now or never! I decided to take the plunge!

THE FIRST ROSEBUD

In 1979 I paid a visit to my banker at First National Bank in Gatesville. I shared with him my plan to open a fine store for ladies. Jack listened politely to my story and said that he would be happy to make the loan I had requested, but he would have to have my husband's signature on the note. I thanked him and left the bank. I had borrowed and paid off a sizable loan with Chase while in the skin care business. I knew that I could count on Chase, but I made the decision to not borrow any money at all. My mother had left me a little money, and I knew she would approve my using it to open The RoseBud.

In the summer of 1979, I was very busy working on my life's dream—a store of my very own! This was so perfect! The building was near the intersection of Highways 36 and 84—a prized location. I leased the white-frame structure featuring two very large French windows facing the intersection. Mr. Bobby Paxton was a great landlord. There was a covered parking area that would be a blessing on rainy days. This was love at first sight, and my creative juices were almost out of control. I wanted my store to be up and running right now!

I always knew that my store, if and when it became a reality, would have bright spring-green carpet, brass fixtures and white wicker furniture. I could hardly wait for the finished product. My

Rosebud Roses

friend Joe came in and spray-painted the walls and raftered ceiling a bright white. The French windows were beautifully draped in sheer white fabric. The lighting fixtures were shiny brass, and the carpet was a lush spring green!

The store was clean, fresh, friendly and comfortable! Garment racks were installed on two walls with over-hanging green canvas awnings. A coffee bar was nestled in the far corner and furnished with white wicker chairs. Cushions in green-and-white print complemented the seating. This little area would serve to entertain many customers.

We had three dressing rooms along one wall, a spacious office area with many built-in filing cabinets and a room for receiving and make-ready tasks. The ladies' room was small but very attractive. This little store was beautiful and very well accepted.

My most treasured fixture was the showcase filled with fabulous accessories. When Dad sold The Leader, I lost claim to the stately claw-foot glass showcase in which I spent my early years creating displays to entice customers. Somehow, it ended up in Jack Kilgore's antique store. I could not wait to drive to Rosebud and buy this fixture. I made sure that it was the first thing customers would see when they entered the shop.

Between the French windows hung a large mirror in an elaborate gold frame. My mother had given me a long marble-top table that I moved from home to the store. It was a perfect fit between the two windows. Charlie and Jack Straw sent an elegant bouquet of gorgeous pink silk roses, which I set on top of the marble table. This little store was meant to warm the hearts of ladies who came to shop. Sometimes we would serve little tea sandwiches, champagne and coffee.

Pink and green were special favorite colors since childhood, so it was no surprise this color scheme followed me through plans for the store. In fact, I still love this combination and even brought it into my home décor.

All my life, I was surrounded by talented family members, and I sincerely loved to help folks look and feel good. Aunt Rose was a model and a merchant. Aunt Pink was a fantastic cook and a master seamstress and clothing designer. Aunt Johnnye was a very talented hairstylist and makeup artist. My mother was all of this and more. She had a fabulous personality and a great love for people. How in the world could I possibly lose?

I say this in all sincerity—I never even thought about the monetary factor. I just wanted to help folks look good and feel good! This was always the primary goal of The RoseBud! I loved my work!

I had some prominent businessmen approach me one day before I opened the store in Gatesville. They offered me the financial backing if I would agree to take their wives to market and allow them to purchase their selections at wholesale costs. Of course, I declined the offer! Did I really look that stupid? Later (much later, in fact), I invited them all to an elegant dinner at Wildflower Country Club in Temple. We had a great time, and it was obvious that they were proud of my accomplishment! I will always have a great respect for these folks!

I was busy putting some finishing touches on the store when Carolyn Davidson stopped in and said, "Betty, I want to work with you." I had not planned on hiring anyone, but Carolyn would be perfect. She was smart, attractive and had a good eye for fashion. Her husband, Cotton, was on Grant Teaff's Baylor coaching staff. Cotton had played football at Baylor before joining a professional team. Carolyn brought lots of friends and acquaintances to the store. She and I were a great team, and we never lost our excitement in the business. She was an ardent shopper and called my attention to a few labels unfamiliar to me.

Rosebud Roses

Naming the store was a top priority. I remember visiting the Tapmans, my brother and sister-in-law, in San Antonio. We were throwing out all kinds of suggestions for naming my life's dream. It suddenly dawned on us that The RoseBud would be perfect. Our Aunt Rose and her husband, Sol Cruvand, started the business in Rosebud, Texas. Our Aunt Pink, the master seamstress, had created fabulous fashions for us ever since birth. The town was Rosebud. Our aunts were named Rose and Pink.

Yes, the name must be The RoseBud, but spelled as one word with a capital "B." The mystery was solved.

My daughter-in-law, Patti, was a teacher in Gatesville, and I was delighted to have her assistance in the opening of The RoseBud. She and I made numerous trips to Dallas while selecting merchandise for the grand opening.

Sharon Meharg and Mary Springstun were two beautiful first-grade teachers who loved fashion. I was delighted to have them as models. They even worked at the store in the summer and on Saturdays. Kelly Miller, a senior at Gatesville High School, was a cheerleader. She was absolutely gorgeous and would be a great model, too. I asked Kelly to model an elegant black cocktail dress by Oscar de la Renta. She was such a beautiful model that we featured her in one of our *Ultra* magazine ads wearing this dress. She was photographed at the entrance to the old Kyle Hotel in Temple. It is a spectacular ad.

The RoseBud in Gatesville, Texas, opened in the early fall of 1979. There was a fabulous cocktail party with live models. Mayor Bob Miller and Bob Thrasher popped the corks on numerous champagne bottles. It was a beautiful evening that I will never, ever forget!

THE YELLOW DIANE VON FURSTENBERG OUTFIT

Carolyn and I were surprised when a new customer arrived at The RoseBud in Gatesville. The lady was obviously beautiful and sophisticated, but her expensive white silk clothes were unkempt, and her blonde hair was needing attention.

The customer selected a few garments very quickly, and I escorted her to a dressing room. When I discovered that she was not wearing undergarments, I explained that we could not allow her to try these items on without wearing panties and a bra.

We suggested that she come back to the store after she cleaned up. She did not seem the least bit offended. She told us that she had been at our courthouse with her significant other while he was being charged with possession of drugs. It was obvious she was a person of class who was very tired and very worried.

We sent her to the Chateau Ville to acquire a room to shower and get some much-needed rest. We also gave her the name of a shop where she could purchase underwear.

A few hours later, she returned to our shop sparkling clean and wearing new underwear, but still in the soiled white silk clothes. We sold her bright-yellow Diane Von Furstenberg jeans and a matching yellow silk Ciao shirt. She was gorgeous.

When I explained that we would need to have identification

Rosebud Roses

and also speak to her Houston bank, she was very accommodating. She purchased quite a few other garments, and her bill was around four thousand dollars. When we called the bank, they let us know that no amount was too large for this lady to handle.

The beautiful lady left our store emphatically praising us for the kindness we had so willingly shown her. Carolyn and I chalked up this situation to a learning experience that we would not soon forget.

HOT PINK AND ORANGE

Mrs. Jim Erwin bought a beautiful mauve-colored Cadillac from Bob, with the understanding that I would drive her and two friends to the Dallas Country Club for a luncheon. The hostess lived in Highland Park, a very exclusive area in Dallas. Her husband was a prominent physician, and their stately two-story home was magnificent. The party at the club was fabulous!

When we arrived at the Dallas Country Club, an elegant party was in progress, honoring a group of debutantes. I will never forget that giant-sized tea table. The hot-pink satin cloth draped to the floor in generous box pleats. The edge of the table was wrapped in wide, orange velvet ribbon, accentuating each corner in a huge bow with streamers cascading to the floor! The enormous centerpiece was a tall cone-shaped base covered in fresh hot-pink roses and real oranges clustered into greenery. Needless to say, I could not get this colorful picture out of my mind!

Some months later, I was called to present a fashion show involving six local stores in Gatesville. I just had to copy that table! It would be the focal setting for the last scene of the show. The tablecloth was fashioned from hot-pink crepe paper. The ribbons were also in crepe paper—bright orange! Of course, the fruit and flowers were artificial, but it was breathtaking.

I dressed a model, Barbara Brown, in a sexy hot-pink-and-orange outfit, dyed her little miniature poodle orange, and sent her to walk the runway with the poodle wearing a little crystal collar on a rhinestone chain. The show was a huge success, and the finale was outstanding.

All of this to say–thanks to Mrs. Erwin. She gave me an opportunity that I will never forget!

PART IV
THE ROSEBUD

"You can do anything you want in life if you dress for it."
—Edith Head

Betty Howe and Lajuan Shelton in Double D Ranchwear at the original Scott & White log cabin; Lexi, Georgia and Kay in silver silk charmeuse at the fountain in the Scott & White entry; Barbara Chandler in Mary Anne Sinclair fashions; high school cheerleader Kelly Miller in Oscar de la Renta.

TAKING THE ROSEBUD TO TEMPLE

The RoseBud in Gatesville was invited to bring a fashion show to King's Daughters Hospital in Temple on a Sunday afternoon. Cheryl Hassman had a delightful deli shop in Temple Mall, so she planned the refreshments and enlisted doctors to don white aprons and chef caps to serve the guests. We all had a fun afternoon, and I felt the event was a huge success, but The RoseBud was never invited back for another show at King's Daughters Hospital.

The Temple Country Club had us present a couple of fashion shows at the Ponderosa. We made many new friends while introducing the Gatesville RoseBud to the area.

Ann Chamlee lived in Temple but had grown up in Gatesville. (Her stepfather was our dentist.) She and Bill had moved to Temple and had many friends. She brought some of them to The RoseBud in Gatesville, and they became regular customers who brought other ladies to shop at the store.

Barbara Goodall and her husband, Dr. Edwin Goodall, were living in Temple while he was recuperating from a severe heart attack. Edwin was working part time at the veterans' hospital, and Barbara was active in the VA Wives Club. Barbara was a vivacious lady who loved fashion and volunteered to work a few hours each week at The RoseBud in Gatesville. I loved having her at the store, and this lady was the start of something great. She insisted that we present a fashion show fundraiser for the VA Wives Club at the City Federation Club House in Temple. Reluctantly, I accepted the challenge. There was immediate response to our show. We began to see ladies from around Central Texas as regular customers at The RoseBud in Gatesville.

Barbara began an immediate campaign to bring The RoseBud to Temple. She came to the shop one day and said, "We need The RoseBud in Temple, Texas! Let's drive over and find a location!" There was a beautiful new two-story building on Loop 363 that looked very promising, and it would have good exposure to the Loop. There was a well-appointed men's store on one corner of the ground level, and it seemed very fitting to have an upscale ladies' boutique on the opposite corner, facing Loop 363.

This did sound exciting, but I needed time to weigh the pros and cons! I asked my friend, J. Don Duncan, a public relations and advertising professional, to run a survey to see if Temple could and would support a store like The RoseBud. The results were an overwhelming positive!

Should I decide to open another store in Temple, I would need help. There was no way I could be in two places at the same time, and this business was very personal. I felt that success would depend on the presence of the owner. So I decided to consult my brother. He suggested that his wife, Charlene, might be interested in becoming a partner in the Temple store. The Tapmans were living in Belton since Tom's retirement from the air force. Charlene accepted the challenge, and I invited her to spend time in the Gatesville store to become familiar with the retail business. Charlene had a background in teaching but had traveled and lived in many different places as an air force wife. She was a fabulous cook and knew how to entertain. So our plans began to take shape.

The rumor spread that The RoseBud might come to Temple, so

Rosebud Roses

we had visits from several Temple bankers seeking our business. We chose Texas Bank, owned by Ernest Fletcher. John Cunningham was president of Texas Bank. We all knew Bill Nesbitt from Gatesville and were aware that he and John had been invited to attend Baylor University on a Citizens National Bank scholarship. (I liked John from our very first visit.) Charlene, Tom and I visited several bankers and decided to go with John at Texas Bank. This was a good decision.

Charlene and I liked the location in Temple's Exchange Plaza and were pleased to find that Elbert Aldrich was one of the owners of the building. (Elbert had graduated from Rosebud High School, and his mother, Mami, had worked for my dad in his store.) So we paid Elbert a visit and laid claim to our new address, 2010 Exchange Plaza, Suite 101, Loop 363, in Temple, Texas. Elbert and his two sons-in-law were wonderful to work with! Rodney later opened his own prestigious real estate business, and after Elbert's death, Lloyd took over the Aldrich-Thomas Group.

Charlene and I set up an appointment with the architect Bill Chamlee. He designed the layout of the store. We loved Bill, and he was wonderful to work with. Since The RoseBud in Gatesville was established and off to a good start, we decided to receive merchandise in Gatesville for the Temple store for the present time. The store was successful right from its beginning (in Gatesville). Things moved swiftly, and J. Don was busy making plans for the formal opening of The RoseBud in Temple, Texas!

Invitations, along with a beautiful long-stemmed pink rose, were hand-delivered to heads of businesses and others we knew. We contacted the Jay Dubose Trio to provide the music and Janis Wright to cater the food. The cocktail party, with live music and real models, was a huge success. We set up an open bar on the checkout counter. The store was completely finished except for placing the merchandise. Models Patti, Sharon, Mary, Sherri and

Tammy, along with our gorgeous professional model from Abilene, paraded through the crowd in elegant outfits for all occasions.

It was a very warm afternoon. The Aldrich family—Elbert, Dorothy Ann, Amy, Lloyd, Ann and Rodney were there. Elbert was perspiring profusely, and I knew that I did not need to say a word! The next day, our air conditioning was superb. This family was delightful, and they took very good care of us. Through all the years we worked with the Aldrich group, our lease was never increased.

The hot weather did not even phase our young master musician, Robert Jeffrey Arnold. He arrived in black tails, white tie and gloves. This handsome, tall and slender gentleman with the beautiful black curly hair was the icing on the cake! He made our party very special! We lost Jeffrey in February 2018 because of a serious automobile accident. He was certainly welcomed into heaven with open arms! We shall miss him terribly.

Charlene Tapman and Betty getting ready for
the opening of The RoseBud in Temple.

THE ROSEBUD ROSE

I had always envisioned this green awning over the entrance to The RoseBud, and it just had to have this perfect pink long-stemmed rose that only one special person could bring to life! So I called my dear friend, Betsi Chamlee, and explained my idea to her. She could see the picture and instantly knew what I had in mind. With a sweep of her magic brush, the perfect rose appeared!

We called on Bill Woodard to reproduce the perfect colors. Bill ran a successful advertising business with an impressive list of clients. We knew that we could count on him to produce the perfect shades of pink for our prestigious rose!

I was beside myself! These people had read my mind! The day this magnificent awning was in its proper place was a great celebration.

This same gorgeous rose was the main attraction on the fabulous billboard on Interstate 35. As I drove toward Temple from Waco and first saw this beautiful billboard, I cried with joy! How in the world could a country girl from a very small town like Rosebud, Texas, receive such a huge honor?

The moral to this story is if we dare to dream long and hard enough, our dreams can come true! My dream began when I was just a young girl growing up in Rosebud, Texas.

This explains the town's motto: Everything is rosy in Rosebud, Texas.

ULTRA

The RoseBud in Temple was up and running full force! We had our first signature advertisement when *Ultra* magazine hit the newsstands and mailboxes the night the Nineteenth Hole opened at Mill Creek Country Club and Golf Course in Salado, Texas. This was an exciting day!

Ultra magazine hosted a cocktail party for their advertisers and friends on the top floor of the Crescent Hotel (before construction was completed) in Dallas. Our advertising manager, J. Don Duncan, Bob and I attended. The two stars of the very popular TV show *Dallas*, J.R. and Sue Ellen, were there. They arrived wearing matching Lynx fur coats and made quite an entrance! Later, Sue Ellen was standing in front of me when it was obvious that her dress was unbuttoned in back. Unconsciously, I proceeded to "fix" the situation (a normal reaction for me), when she turned and gave me a "look"! When I explained what I was doing, she gave me a rather weak smile. She looked very coarse up close, which was surprising. She was flawlessly beautiful on TV!

Patti Thrasher in Oscar de la Renta for
The RoseBud's first *Ultra* ad.

THE HOT-PINK DRESS

I sold a magnificent dress to Margaret Brown, a prominent lady in a neighboring town. The color was a bright, vibrant hot pink. The full skirt of cut-work embroidered silk emphasized the tiny waist. A soft, rounded neckline and elbow-length sleeves were perfect balance for this bouffant skirt. Margaret and her husband, Spencer, were known for the elegant parties in their tasteful home. They were a handsome couple. He was a successful businessman, and she was a brilliant and beautiful hostess.

One day, a customer came into The RoseBud and wanted the very same dress in the identical color. I tactfully explained that I could not sell this dress to her. I explained that the two women lived in the same town, and it was a store policy to protect such purchases. This woman simply was not prepared to accept my reasoning. After quite a few alternate solutions and discussions about the best styles and colors for her, she agreed to accept my choices. She left the store as happy as a lark. All it took was a little patience and proper guidance.

GEORGE W. BUSH

When George W. Bush was running for president, Bob and I attended a reception in his honor. It was a huge affair with hundreds of people attending.

As we inched our way through the long line to greet our future president, we enjoyed the people and struck up some interesting conversations. When we finally reached the guest of honor to shake his hand, he said, "Well hello, Betty. It is so good to see you. Thanks for coming." I was impressed!

Later, I said to Bob, "I wonder how George Bush knew my name."

Bob replied with a big, robust laugh, "Silly. You were wearing a name tag!"

Our family loves the Bushes, and we have such respect for them. George and Laura are so kind and compassionate. They are still showing up in all the right places to show their love and concern for the folks in America.

THE NAVY CRYSTAL CREATION

The dress was a simple masterpiece that would require the perfect lady. The exquisite dark-navy sheer lace was lavishly sprinkled with Swarovski crystals from Austria that sparkled like stars in the night sky. The jewel neck and long, fitted sleeves were the perfect companions to the slender ankle-length sheath. The dress had its own navy silk charmeuse slip. The only accessories needed were diamond earrings and matching high-heeled strappy satin sandals. This was a special order for a delightful, petite lady who came for her fitting.

The dress was way too long, and at this time, we had not found our in-store alteration lady, so the search was on for the one best suited for this job. She came to us highly recommended. The length must be shortened. When it was returned, and the customer came to try on the dress, it was a disaster. It was much shorter on one side. The customer could not leave the store with her dress. We called the designer and asked them to make another identical dress. They were more than willing to accommodate us and made the dress the perfect length for our customer.

We could not return the dress with the botched hem, and we could not sell this dress in the area. What could we do? Gini's husband was a general in the army, stationed in our area. She was the perfect size to fit the dress. It was possible to even the hem to serve as an ankle-length formal gown. We found the alteration lady who could make our dream come true.

Gini was absolutely gorgeous in the dress. It looked like it was made for her. She and the general were a stunning couple. We gave Gini the dress as a gift. She and her handsome husband were off to a new assignment. We were happy to send them off in style.

ON THE STREET CORNER IN NEW YORK CITY

While patiently standing on a New York City street corner, waiting for the traffic light to change, Marion and Bill Brakebill struck up a conversation with an attractive lady and asked if she would recommend a good restaurant for dinner. She asked where they were from. When Bill said, "Temple, Texas," she was excited and asked if they knew Betty Thrasher. As the three of them walked on, they had fun discussing The RoseBud in Temple, Texas. The lady just happened to be a person we did business with in New York City.

It's such a small world!

A PERFECT FIT

We have many great stories to tell about the customer service at The RoseBud. It was our privilege to have been of service.

A customer from New York City contacted The RoseBud about a dress in one of our *Ultra* magazine ads. She requested a size ten. We were unable to get this size because this particular style was sold out. We did have one size eight in the store, so we altered this dress, extending the waist and bust to size ten. We explained our plan to the customer and assured her that we would gladly take the dress back if she was not pleased. We shipped the dress to a Fifth Avenue address in New York City. The dress fit perfectly, and she was elated! Everyone was happy, and the alteration lady, Elsie, was the star.

The RoseBud had a very special mission. The purpose of this unique business was to serve as a personal adviser to women who want to be advised as to lines and shapes and designs and fabrics that are most flattering to their body type. All of these features should be considered in order to obtain the best results. Color is a subject to be taught! Most women have favorite colors. Some folks have been told what colors are good for them and what colors they should never wear. Many have been told they cannot wear black! I beg to disagree! Everyone can wear black—which, incidentally, is fashion's number one color! What a shame it would be to go through life never enjoying the privilege of wearing black.

Professional model from Abilene at the opening of The RoseBud in Temple.

THE CHRISTMAS BREAK-IN

The call came about four a.m. The police said The RoseBud had been broken into and that the glass doors were shattered. Everything was fine when we left the store about 6:30 p.m.

It was two days before Christmas. We had enjoyed great response from our trunk show that week. Only three furs and an Ultrasuede suit with a fox collar were left to deliver on Christmas Eve. And, of course, these would be paid for on delivery. These four items were all that were missing. My partner, Charlene, and I did not personally own furs. This merchandise was not insured. This was a sad day at The RoseBud. We had learned a huge lesson.

Our alarm worked. It took police less than two minutes to reach the store. The weapon used to break the glass doors was an iron tire tool the burglars left behind without fingerprints.

We were disappointed our four customers had a sad Christmas without their special gifts!

LITTLE MODELS

Katie Dunn

I adored my little models through the years of The RoseBud's runway shows. Katie Dunn began modeling before she started first grade. Dillard's in the Temple Mall was kind enough to accommodate us when we chose to use children or men in our shows. The RoseBud only catered to women's fashions.

On one such occasion, Katie would be modeling several outfits with her mother, Ann. On this particular day, we were getting set up for a show at the Frank Mayborn Convention Center. Katie was wearing a little scotch-plaid pleated skirt and cable sweater with a matching tam. She had her tiny black reading glasses on when she looked over the rim of them and said, "Betty, I will need a desk, so I can study better between changes." Of course, we immediately attended to her request.

Katie even modeled for us when she was at Baylor University. She gave me a precious picture of herself in a Baylor Homecoming parade, framed in tiny pink porcelain roses.

The RoseBud dressed the mothers of both the bride and groom for Katie's marriage to David. It was a gorgeous wedding, nothing less than one would expect from such sweet, talented people.

David went to medical school and became a physician like

his dad. They are an outstanding couple with two precious little daughters.

The Mullins Twins

Mary Helen and Sally were the little daughters of Melissa and Pat Mullins. They are still gorgeous, identical twins with handsome husbands and beautiful children. Mary Helen and Tyler Johnson have two little sons. Sally and Lee Armstrong have two little girls.

They were just little girls when we invited the twins to model in one of our big runway shows benefiting Scott & White Hospital. They were wearing bright-yellow raincoats with matching hats and rain boots. Each one carried an open umbrella. They were not at all excited about this assignment. In fact, they just plain did not want to do this. They cried real tears all the way down the runway, providing their very own raindrops, and, of course, they stole the whole show!

We'll never forget this! They made the day, and we love these beautiful ladies and their precious families.

THE SYMPHONY BELLE

I was called to jury duty, and during a break, I heard over the loud speaker, "Mrs. Betty Thrasher, the judge would like to see you in his chambers." I was shaking like a leaf. I slowly maneuvered into his office.

Judge Bob Cummings said, "How are you today, Betty?" Well, truthfully, I wasn't doing so well, and then the Judge said, "Betty, our daughter, Meredith, is a Symphony Belle, and she is needing a special formal dress." I managed to regain my composure and tell the judge that The RoseBud could certainly handle his request.

The judge's lovely wife, Joy, and their beautiful brunette daughter came over to Temple, and we decided on a gorgeous red formal and had a famous designer, Victor Costa, make this special dress.

When the dress was delivered, it lacked six inches closing at the back. The company had miscalculated the measurements. Time was running close, so we had Victor send us extra fabric. Our miracle seamstress, Elsie, worked her magic needle, and the dress was a perfect fit for our Cinderella. We were happy to be invited to the presentation in Waco. We were very proud of our Meredith. She was gorgeous, and the dress was perfect. Thank you, Elsie!

THE JET SET

This Houston couple was coming to The RoseBud to select the wardrobe for the wife, who was about to launch her own television show. The petite lady, Pat, was first off the plane, followed by her husband. He was dressed in striped overalls with white tennis shoes. We drove them to The RoseBud.

With approval from her husband, Pat selected several suits, dresses and formal gowns. She wore my shoe size, so we added the perfect footwear to each outfit. The husband's approval was obvious. The very last garment we sold them was a full-length mink coat dyed blue! This was her favorite color, so it was added to the wardrobe without hesitation.

The husband wanted the shoes also. I explained that the shoes were my personal possession and that I could not sell them but offered to purchase new ones from Cinderella shoe store in Waco. He was delighted, so I called Doyle Moody and placed the order. He shipped the shoes directly to her in Houston.

Our alteration lady made the necessary adjustments to the clothing items, carefully packed the garments and shipped them to Pat. The couple was overwhelmed with the service and attention they received from The RoseBud. They became regular customers.

Wes Gilbreath Sr. was the owner of SignAd in Houston. He wrote a very interesting book, *The Road Out of Town Is a Two-Way Street*.

THE FUR COAT

The RoseBud partnership was dissolved in the early 1990s, and I assumed complete ownership of the business. We had some fun times as partners, and the valuable experiences gained through these ten years will never be forgotten. Lifelong friendships were developed and cherished. We were blessed.

The next years were bursting with excitement and new growing pains. The staff at The RoseBud was the best! Each person who worked with the group added a new dimension to the business. Our full-time employees could be found mostly in the office and our stockroom. The part-time sales and fashion advisers were pillars of the community, highly respected by our loyal customers. We all had the same goal in mind. Our pledge was to provide the best service on the planet for everyone who entered our doors. Customers had their favorite adviser, and we always honored their requests. Herb Chaffin stopped me one time and said, "I was not a frequent visitor to The RoseBud, but you had such a wonderful group of ladies in your store." I appreciated this comment more than Herb could imagine. I recall, with great appreciation, the day he came in and purchased a magnificent lynx coat for his daughter—not for show, but because she lived in a very cold climate. What a sweet thing to do.

Fur shows were always exciting. Most women would dream of

owning a beautiful fur, and even if it did not seem so practical to own one, it was a treat to just come to The RoseBud and try on furs. I will never forget when I bought a fur jacket for myself. I was modeling for Mr. Jack's in Waco. He was having a fur show. I do not know what possessed me to buy that autumn haze fur jacket, but I was so glad I did. It was early fall, and of course, in Texas, it was still quite warm.

My young son, Michael, questioned my motive and wondered where and when I would get to wear this warm, fuzzy friend. I assured him that in spite of my purchase, he would still be going to college one day. This seemed to satisfy his curiosity.

One of the most memorable times I got to wear my autumn haze mink jacket was when Corinne Erwin and I decided to get a foursome together one evening. None of us had a washing machine, so we depended on a local washeteria to do our weekly wash. We had the most fun evening wearing our furs, doing our wash and drinking cokes while playing bridge at our favorite washeteria. Seriously, we loved it.

IN-STORE THEFT

On a crisp, cool morning, I came to work from Gatesville to find a group of friends and customers having coffee in our corner seating area. I usually went directly to the office to shed coat, purse and any other items before going out on the floor to greet customers and employees. Today was different, as I stopped to visit and deposited my handbag on the seat of a big chair.

A couple entered the store, and the lady shopped for a coat. Her husband was observing, and he took one of the coats and carefully placed it over the back of the chair where I had placed my handbag. Shortly after, I picked up the handbag and proceeded to my office. For some reason, I needed my billfold. When I reached into my bag, it was not there! I ran out of the office just as the couple was driving away but managed to get their license number! I knew the billfold was in my bag when I left home, and my only stop was The RoseBud. I could now plainly see the man gently placing the coat over the back of the chair and my handbag. So I called the police!

That evening when I was at home in Gatesville, a friend called. She had been shopping in a Waco mall when a woman attempted to use my credit card. Somehow, she heard my name called and spoke up to say, "I know Betty Thrasher, and this lady is not her!"

The woman ran, with security in pursuit, but got away outside and jumped into the waiting vehicle.

A couple of months later, I was in a store across the Loop from The RoseBud when I recognized the man who had been in my store the day my billfold went missing! I located a security guard and alerted him to this person and my experience. Then I went over to the thief and let him know that I knew he had taken the billfold.

In the meantime, I had a call from a liquor store in Lacy Lakeview, just north of Waco, wanting to know why I had stopped payment on a three-hundred-dollar-plus check! That check and eight hundred dollars in cash had been in the billfold! These thieves had made other purchases with my credit card and had gotten away with the crime! These places of business evidently had not asked for ID. So, when someone asks for you to verify your identity, remember, that it is for *your* protection!

This was a real eye-opener for me! I learned to never let my credentials leave my sight! It really is better to be safe than sorry!

THE DISGRUNTLED CUSTOMER

A lady from Austin, Texas, arrived at The RoseBud one morning. She was obviously not excited to be here. She let me know she had no intentions of being impressed with anything we attempted to show her. My job was to change her attitude. After a short visit in our seating area, she began to settle down, warm up to our hospitality and decide The RoseBud was a very special store after all.

We never know the circumstances that can put a person into such a negative attitude, but with just a little sincere, calming attention, we can turn things around. It was fun to have coffee and conversation with this lady. The longer we visited, the more relaxed she became.

I loved showing her items that I felt would best complement her lifestyle. She was very receptive to my suggestions and agreed to progress to a fitting room. In the end, she made the selections of items that appealed to her. She was having a good time!

The customer invested about $4,500 in her purchases. She left The RoseBud with a smile on her face. She turned out to be a very regular customer and a wonderful new friend.

As she left the store, she gave me a hug and said that she had loved the visit. Her last words were, "I needed this!"

We never know what the other person has had happen in her life. But there is one thing I am sure of: a cup of coffee, a good listener and to know the person cares is good medicine for whatever ails us!

TEMPLE'S NORTHSIDE

Temple's Northside was the elite address. I was first introduced to this sacred area as a junior high student in Rosebud when Mary Jane Sapp and I visited Teenie Chernoskey in Temple. Teenie's dad was a doctor at King's Daughters Hospital. His sister, Miss Annie Chernoskey, lived in Rosebud. She was an accomplished pianist who had studied in Europe. Jane and I were her students. Dr. Chernoskey and my mother grew up together in Rosebud.

During these visits to Temple, we met many of Teenie's friends—Errol Wendland, Ernest Fletcher, Carolyn Culp, the Snodgrass twins and Rae Virginia McCreary. My distant relatives, the Charles Zidell family, also lived here. My family also knew the Hendlers. (The Zidells and Hendlers had clothing stores in Temple.)

Many years later, when The RoseBud opened in Temple (1981), we became good friends with the fabulous Northside Ladies—Martha Jean Burleson, Robbie Culp, Corrinne Daniel, Cleo and Joan Brindley, Doris Floca, Frances Secrest and Alene White. Martha Jean was belle of the ball and eventually came to work part-time at The RoseBud.

Mary Purifoy and Joy Farris were close friends who also lived on the Northside. These two gorgeous ladies were recognized everywhere by their beautiful white hair and outgoing personalities.

They walked The RoseBud runways on a regular basis, and Mary joined our staff as a sales associate and popular fashion advisor.

Rosemary Mullins had three wonderful sons, Bob, Michael and Pat, who were as different as night and day. Bob is an avid outdoor enthusiast, like his dad, Moon. Patrick is a very successful businessman, who wed gorgeous Melissa Heap. Melissa Heap Mullins is a real beauty inside and out! She and her children modeled for The Rosebud when we could catch her in town. She and Pat travel frequently and are always planning exciting family getaways.

Michael is a worldly character with loads of talent. He is a world traveler, extremely well-read and very talented in many fields. We became acquainted when Michael was a vice president of Fashion Center Dallas. His personality made the place click. All three brothers are respected and dearly loved.

Michael is working on a documentary on the highly recognized fashion expert, Stanley Marcus. Michael is closely associated with his alma mater, TCU. The university recently honored him, along with several others, at a luncheon. Michael eats, sleeps and lives the color purple. This guy just lights up a room the moment he enters.

The mother of these three sons, Rosemary, was a Kilgore Rangerette back in her college days. The originator of this fantastic precision drill team lived in an apartment close to Rosemary's home. Her boys always thought Gussie Nell Davis was their aunt.

BAYLOR ADVISORY BOARD

Dr. Judith Lusk invited me to sit on an advisory board at Baylor University. We opened the doors of The RoseBud to Baylor students studying fashion design and marketing, in order for them to learn firsthand about quality, workmanship, fabrics and sales. We had about twelve students serve as dressers for our most exciting fashion shows. This would allow them to observe the final touch to each outfit on The RoseBud runways. I enjoyed many years of close connection to the students and faculty of Baylor University along with my daughter-in-law, Patti. Students were exposed to fashionable casual, daywear, semiformal, formal and couture clothing. We even had some of the student designers show their creations at our RoseBud shows.

SHOPPING IN WACO

Shopping trips to Waco meant getting all dressed up—heels, hats and gloves! We usually had lunch at the Piccadilly Cafeteria on Austin Avenue. Bauer-McCann was a lovely store, but for some reason, we rarely shopped there.

Cinderella was known for beautiful shoes and Mr. Doyle Moody, who never forgot a customer's size or style and color preference. *Texas Monthly* magazine paid him a true compliment when they did a feature story on Doyle, entitled "Prince of Pumps." I bought my first pair of dressy heels at Cinderella. When the Cinderella store on New Road closed, it was like a funeral all over the state of Texas.

Zales Jewelers was a popular place. My parents bought silver tea services for each of us. Izzy Fred was a friend of my dad's. My sister and I each had a diamond ring from Zales, a gift from our parents. Izzy was a special friend of Walter Baker, superintendent of the Bremond Schools, who was married to Bob's sister, Grace. The Freds loved Baylor University, and the feeling was mutual.

Mr. Jack's was famous for the elegant bridal shop. Mrs. Graham was a very petite, fashionable lady who wore her salt-and-pepper hair swept up in a very sophisticated chignon. She knew what she was doing and not a single bride questioned her opinion. Mr. Jack's exclusive ladies' store was under the direction of Doris Meyer, who dressed many of the prominent ladies in Waco. Each season, she would select complete wardrobes for her regular customers. I considered both Graham and Doris very special friends.

Aubrey and Charlotte opened a very elite ladies' boutique on Austin Avenue. Sach's was a plush store that women over Texas liked to patronize. There were elaborate glass mannequin cases on the sidewalk in front of the store. It looked like New York City! The Sachs were very knowledgeable on the subject of fashion. I took my sister there to select her wedding gown and part of her *trousseau*. When the store closed, I was very honored when Charlotte brought many of her customers to The RoseBud in Temple.

Cox's Department Store was located in Westview Village on Valley Mills Drive. This was a great store! Our boys, Bobby and Mike, loved to shop at Cox's. They had the first escalator in Waco, and this was quite an attraction. Clothing for men, women and children were just some of the features. The shoe and household departments were outstanding also. I bought Bob a pair of black lizard loafers, and he wore them for years. They were extremely comfortable and never looked worn. I paid $225 for them and thought that was expensive.

Goldstein-Migel was the most elaborate department store in Waco and between Dallas and Austin. I never knew the namesakes, but Monty Lawrence was a strikingly handsome man with the most perfect posture I had ever seen. He was tall and always immaculately dressed. Abby and Ann Freed, a beautiful couple, could be seen scurrying around the store adding their magic touch.

This store featured a glamorous fur salon and bridal shop. The store was quite elegant and was the main anchor for Lake Air Mall on Bosque Avenue. Their beauty salon was very popular among women in the area. My friend, Ross Coskrey, was a prominent hairstylist there until he opened his own shop, Parkdale Salon.

When Goldstein-Migel closed, it brought a feeling of great

Rosebud Roses

sadness to everyone far and near. Once again, I was humbled when Ann Freed brought her customers to The RoseBud in Temple. Occasionally, Ann would bring her husband, Abby, when she came to shop. Sometimes, we would go to Wildflower Country Club for lunch and talk "shop." When this business gets into someone's blood, they are hooked for life.

Holt's had a sporting goods store in downtown Waco when they opened a ready-to-wear store in Lake Air Mall. Later, they added My, Oh, My, a specialty store, and Wanda Fannin was the manager. Some years later, Wanda visited The RoseBud in Temple and told us that she was opening a wonderful store in Waco. Our dear friend, Carol Thompson, modeled for her. Carol's husband, Rickie, grew up next door to us in Gatesville. He played football at Baylor and, later, with the Washington Redskins. Rickie was now a prominent banker in Waco. He and Michael are still friends. Rick's new bank and Michael's new dental office are located very near each other in Woodway.

Sam Harlick's prestigious men's store in Lake Air Mall was a huge favorite of business and college men. Sam was a master of the business. When our son, Michael, was a student at Baylor, we went to Sam for the perfect outfit for interviews with Baylor University and Baylor Dental School.

Sam chose a beautiful black-and-white glen plaid suit with just a hint of red. The white dress shirt fabric was gorgeous. He selected a black silk tie with a row of tiny red roses running diagonally across the center. Michael wore this outfit before a panel of five judges at Baylor University. The men commented on his spectacular outfit and asked where he purchased it. Sam told us that three of the men came to his store to shop and complimented Sam on Mike's choices. Michael wore the same ensemble for his interview at Baylor Dental in Dallas. Our young son was on his way to success.

Betty Thrasher

    I have a special fondness for Baylor University, where Michael graduated cum laude before being accepted to Baylor Dental School in Dallas. Coach Art Briles of Baylor University has my great admiration for what he accomplished in their football program, and I am excited by the outstanding basketball program for both the men and women.

GOOD FRIENDS AND BUSINESS RELATIONSHIPS AROUND WACO

We have been blessed with many experiences of great value in Waco. We have so many good friends there. Back when my dad caught a huge bass in Rosebud City Lake, we rushed to Pure Milk Company in Waco, where his friend, Frank Matthews, greeted us and froze the fish in ice. It could then be displayed at Padget's sporting goods store. Frank Matthews and Young Smith were fishing buddies of my dad's.

Dr. F. William Hohen was our boys' pediatrician. He had a huge dog who curled up on the rug in his office. So, for safety's sake, one did whatever the doctor suggested. We were regular visitors while the boys were growing up.

Dr. Nick Bellegie was an outstanding surgeon who worked in Gatesville on special cases with Doctors Ellsworth and Wendell Lowrey. We became friends with this wonderful doctor. He was a customer of Bob's.

Rick Vela had a special talent in the field of men's clothing, and he was an excellent golfer. I bought Bob a gorgeous pair of off-white wool gaberdine trousers, and they still hang in Bob's closet.

Many years later the slacks look the same as when new. Rick was a stickler for quality fabric. He and Bob played several golf tournaments.

Piazza Shoe Repair always welcomed us with a big smile. We needed the special talents that this business offered so we could keep our favorite footwear in first-class condition. There are some things we just don't find easy to discard. The folks at Piazza made old boots and shoes look like new.

Jimmy and Juanita Willis were among the best photographers in the country. We have wonderful gold-framed photos of each of our sons—Bobby and Michael—at age three. After Bobby's photo, we saved his clothes until Michael was three years old. The Willises photographed the boys facing each other. They advised me to take away the collared white shirt and replace it with a simple white Buster Brown T-shirt. The wheat-colored linen jacket with pearl buttons was much more appealing with emphasis on these two darling faces instead of the big, open-collared white shirt. This was very good advice.

Folks in the Jewish community will always be close to my heart. So many of them were wonderful customers at The RoseBud in Temple. I did a few fashion shows for Hadassah at the Brazos Club. I enjoyed visiting with Arnold and Yvonne Miller. Arnold was very knowledgeable on the subject of fashion. I loved visiting with David Hoppenstein while Lorraine shopped. David graduated from Baylor and Baylor Law School and attended Harvard Law School, so we had many topics to discuss. The Hoppensteins have cemetery lots across the road from ours. My family members, Aunt Rose and Uncle Sol Cruvand, Aunt Dora Swartz and my dad, Harry M. Tapman, are buried just inside the gate of the entrance to the cemetery. Someday, I want to walk through this cemetery with my children and tell them about my friends who are resting there.

PENNY RICHARDS

Penny Richards was a frequent customer at The RoseBud who had excellent taste and an appreciation for quality. We were privileged to meet her fashion desires for many special occasions. Daughter Terri was honored upon graduation with a glamorous party at 25th Street Theater. Beautiful photos of Terri greeted guests as they entered amid roving beams lighting up the sky and two great rock bands keeping time to the occasion. Terri's outfit featured glittering stars on black and white. She was beautiful!

Penny was there when the tall ships sailed into the harbor of New York City. Her gown featured the beaded skyline of the city that never sleeps!

The RoseBud dressed ladies of all ages for the celebrated Cotton Palace pageant each year in Waco, Texas. This was a very prestigious affair in this city.

MAMIE SUE AT THE ORGAN

Mamie Sue Hallbrook was a middle school teacher who played the organ at First Methodist Church in Gatesville. She came to me in search of a Sunday dress. My thought was to first consider the undergarments for this teacher, who had obvious posture needs. I fitted her in a one-piece undergarment that insisted that she sit up straight. The dress was a smart navy-blue fitted style with a flattering portrait collar. She looked fabulous, and her overall body shape was perfect. As she gazed at her reflection in the full-length mirror, I could feel her approval.

On Sunday morning, despite the fact that she wore no makeup, Mamie Sue looked magnificent sitting on the bench before the massive organ. My chest swelled with pride. On Monday morning, she came to me and said, "I could hardly breathe and felt like I might even pass out. The undergarment has to go. I cannot tolerate this discomfort."

We've always heard that sometimes we have to suffer to be beautiful, but in this case, we had to agree with Mamie Sue. She had allowed herself to slump. To heck with good posture!

THE GRANDMOTHER'S LAST DRESS

The thirteen-year-old girl, accompanied by two ladies, did all the talking when she came into The RoseBud in a desperate search for a special dress. The color had to be pink. The dress was for her grandmother, who had passed away. The little girl tried hard to hold back the tears, and it was quite obvious that the two ladies were in sympathy with her.

She explained that a dress had been purchased at the mall, but the girl was not pleased with it. "This dress has to be beautiful," she said.

So I opened the mirrored doors to reveal the closet for our best special occasion garments. We thumbed through the selections until we caught sight of an elegant soft-pink silk jacquard dress. I took it from the closet and said, "Could this be the one?" The tag was marked $400. The ladies told the girl that this was above their budget. I saw the disappointment in her face.

"But this dress is for my grandmother, and she should have a special dress for this occasion," said the girl.

I stood there feeling rather helpless as I remembered losing my own grandmother when I was about this child's age, and I could feel her pain. This was just too much to let go. Right then, I made the decision as I said, "How about The RoseBud making this dress a gift to you in honor of your grandmother?" The little girl burst into tears, and the ladies lost their composure, too. We all had a good cry as I asked one of the employees to put the dress in one of our RoseBud bags.

I did not know these people, but I was feeling their loss as I went to the visitation at the funeral home but did not sign the register. The little girl was right. Their pretty grandmother deserved a gorgeous dress for this very special occasion. And I felt like the weight of the world had been lifted from my shoulders. It really is true: it is better to give than receive.

THE FORGIVING WAISTLINE

Doris Floca, a prominent Northside lady, came to The RoseBud in search of the perfect dress for her granddaughter's wedding. We didn't seem to have what she had in mind. We were always prepared to do whatever was needed in order to please our customers. So I offered to call Neiman Marcus in Dallas to see if they had the right dress for her.

As we get a little more comfortable with the years, we seem to add a little extra baggage to the midsection. I called the store in Dallas and explained that we were searching for a beautiful dress with a "forgiving" waistline. The lady said that Neiman's had no such garment. I proceeded to call the Houston store and got the same reply. So I sent Doris and her daughter to a store in Austin that seemed to understand the style I was talking about. The ladies came by The RoseBud on their return from Austin. The store did not have the dress we were searching for.

I suggested that I had a dress in stock that would be the perfect answer to our situation, but it was way too much dress for little Doris, who was just a might too petite for the garment I had in mind. We decided to have her slip on the dress and called in the alteration expert to see if it would be possible to remake the dress to our satisfaction. Elsie Springer went to work with her magic pin tray and measuring tape, and right before our very eyes, the beautiful George F. Couture formal gown was created for our special lady! Doris looked so gorgeous at her granddaughter's magnificent wedding. The RoseBud had done it again.

Shortly after this wedding, I was attending the Dallas market. My friend Phyllis was having a fabulous dinner party in her lovely North Dallas home. She asked if I would host the dining room guests, while she would serve in the same capacity in the great room where others would be seated overlooking the brilliant lighting of the pool. It was such a beautiful party, and everyone had a great time.

My friend from New York, D'Arcy, was seated next to me. Across the table sat a very distinguished-looking couple. We were all involved in the fashion business. Some of the guests were store owners while others were buyers, designers and manufacturers. Needless to say, we all spoke the same language.

I decided to tell the story about Doris's dress. I described the phone conversations with the Neiman stores while I was in search of a dress featuring the forgiving waistline and was told each time that Neiman's did not carry such a garment. All the time I was recounting my story, D'Arcy was attempting to get my attention by tapping on my leg! I did not get the picture, so I said, "D'Arcy, what do you want?"

She calmly said, "Betty, the lady across from you is the couture buyer for Neiman Marcus stores."

My reaction, without even thinking about it, was, "Well, ma'am, you need to hear this story so your salespeople understand the definition of a forgiving waistline."

She looked at me, and we both smiled, and she said, "Indeed. I do need to pass this information on to our sales staff."

It is obvious that as we age, some of us have the tendency to lose that tiny waistline, while, at the same time, we may be accumulating more financial status. Stores like Neiman's obviously have such customers, and I am quite sure that their needs and wishes are met. It was just a play on words that got in the way! Today, even the most perfect figures love the blouson or dropped-waist designs, and it has absolutely nothing to do with the figure. Life is just a study on many various subjects.

Betty wearing the forgiving waistline dress.

POLLY PARNELL

Polly Parnell is a dear friend and a remarkable lady. To be in this lady's company is a special treat. She and her husband, Ben (who is deceased), have enjoyed living on a beautiful ranch in the Little River-Academy area. As one gazes through the windows of the breakfast room, there stands a gorgeous grove of trees, a perfect place to go for meditation or to daydream on a crisp fall day. This setting is so peaceful!

Polly has a wonderful family. Every one of them is smart and successful. They are fun to be with on any occasion—a casual visit or very special event. Polly is well-known for her delicious homemade bread that she generously shares with her many friends.

Ben was a successful banker and a brilliant man. Their daughter Jeanie followed in her dad's footsteps and was honored as the outstanding banker in San Antonio before her retirement. Their son, Rob, is a successful businessman in Dallas.

REPUBLICAN WOMEN'S SHOW IN AUSTIN

Clayton Williams was running for governor of the great state of Texas, and Rob Mosbacher was his running mate for lieutenant governor. I certainly was not into politics so, needless to say, I was not at all aware of the fact that the models who were sent to us for fittings were actually celebrities. When the Polo Shop called to inquire if I would read their script, I said, "No, I do not read notes for my shows. I prefer to just talk about the fashions as they come down the runway. But, if I can view the clothes and meet your models before the show, I will be delighted to do my best in properly presenting your fashions from the Polo Shop." I was very unaware of the prominence of their models. The gentlemen were all handsome. I should have been embarrassed when I referred to one young man as "Honey." How in the world was I to know that he just happened to be the secretary of state?

Overall, the show was fantastic, and all the models were magnificent. The fashions were outstanding, and the models performed like pros. It seemed as if we had all worked together many times before.

We took our own makeup and hairstylist teams with us. The RoseBud loved having the Lancôme makeup artists from Temple Mall Dillard's, led by Angela Allen and Gaylene Galloway. Karen

Dungan was the lead hairstylist from Fountain of Beauty. These ladies are very fine professionals. They provide the most important accessories in the world of fashion.

The clothes were outstanding. The RoseBud models were perfect. The show went off without a hitch. Since the sponsor was the Republican Women's Club of Austin, we planned to end on a patriotic note, covering every look and occasion. Garments in the colors of red, white and blue filled the runway. There was a red cashmere jogging suit, a very formal beaded gown in sapphire and an elegant full-length white mink coat and matching floppy brimmed hat with a touch of leopard. We covered every look for every occasion to the tunes of "The Eyes of Texas" and "God Bless America."

The capacity crowd honored us with a rousing standing ovation. We were honestly blessed to have the opportunity to meet many outstanding people and personalities.

Katherine Mosbacher was a dream to work with and so easy to fit. Everything looked great on her. When Rob Mosbacher was in town, he would stop by The RoseBud to say hello.

Jane Sibley modeled in our show but was unable to come to Temple to be fitted. We selected several outfits for her, and when we arrived in Austin, we had her try them. They were perfect, and she showed them well. Our show could not have been more spectacular and well-received.

Clayton Williams came backstage to personally thank everyone. Mrs. Williams, Modesta, was a star. She is a gorgeous lady who wears clothes like a million dollars. Modesta Williams came back and modeled in one of our Scott & White shows. The crowd adored her!

Modesta Williams on the runway at the Republican Women's Club of Austin fashion show.

THE RIGHT PLACE AT THE RIGHT TIME

The RoseBud was an attraction in Temple where friends could meet and visit without feeling pressured to make a purchase. Men felt comfortable to stop by after a tennis match or a round of golf. The coffee was always fresh, and the cokes were cold. When gift suggestions were needed, our staff could deliver impeccable customer service. Our clientele knew they could count on us. It was our mission to be sure that every gift was perfect for the receiver. It always pays to know one's customers. Mistakes can be costly.

We loved to have the men accompany their ladies on shopping trips to The RoseBud. Many children grew up accompanying moms to our store. Impressions were made early on to last for years to come. Linda Ringler was one of our favorite customers who agreed to model for The RoseBud in our fashion shows. One day her grown-up son, Donnie, came in and told us he had been to the mall shopping for a gift for his mom when he realized that he was in the wrong place. It suddenly dawned on him that the ladies at The RoseBud would have the best suggestion. Donnie said, "Mrs. Thrasher, I can't believe I wasted so much time when The RoseBud would have the perfect answer." And sure enough, his gift thrilled his mom.

Rosebud Roses

Drayton McLane dropped his boys off at The RoseBud to select a gift for their mom, Elizabeth. He gave me a credit card and said he would pick the boys up in forty-five minutes. They made their selection, and we dressed their gift in our signature pink moiré paper, satin ribbon and long-stemmed silk rose. This was a good experience for the McLane boys—Drayton III and Denton. This dad was giving his sons an important lesson.

Garlyn Shelton stopped by one day and left money for Lajuan's scheduled shopping trip to The RoseBud. She was delighted with this surprise, and Garlyn had said, "If she selects something more expensive, give me a call."

Jack Elam, an Evant banker, asked me to bring some furs to his bank for his wife, Kathryn, and daughter, Linda Kay, to select. We had so much fun, and the ladies loved their coats.

Judge Jack Prescott got a thrill when he chose gifts for Betty, the love of his life. We called them the Cinderella Couple. I can only recall one time that Betty exchanged a gift from Jack. She was always pleased with our recommendations.

A prominent San Antonio businessman was a patient at Scott & White. On his many visits for scheduled appointments, he would purchase a gift for his wife. We knew her well, so I cannot recall her exchanging a gift that he purchased at The RoseBud.

There was one customer who always wanted to purchase a gift for his Scott & White contact who scheduled his appointments. He would ask us to select an item, gift wrap it in our signature silk rose package and deliver it to the hospital. She never received one of these gifts that she did not return. We tried very hard to teach her about good quality, but we never felt like we had succeeded. This was disappointing. I've been told that we just can't win them all!

Grandsons Jeffery Todd Thrasher and Aaron Michael Thrasher enjoying a champagne toast at the twenty-fifth anniversary of The RoseBud.

WEDDINGS

The Breakers

    We had a lady drive six hundred miles from her Texas ranch to The RoseBud! Her daughter was marrying an heir to a prominent department store chain. I was amazed that she did not shop at this family's store, which was very well known and prestigious, too! The wedding would take place at the Breakers Hotel in Palm Beach, Florida—a beautiful oceanfront resort! This is one of the legendary oceanfront resorts in North America, energized by a genuinely caring staff that offers guests everything under the sun!

    This mother of the bride purchased an entire wardrobe, including the accessories. She selected some of our finest pieces from France, plus a few items fitting for her ranch-style life! We were extremely proud of her selections! She stayed in Temple overnight, and the next morning we loaded her purchases into her SUV and off she went! She was delighted with what The RoseBud had to offer!

Mother of the Bride

    A customer from Dallas called for an appointment on a Saturday morning. I did not know her, so I had nothing to analyze before she came to The RoseBud that day! When they arrived, the daughter was with her, wearing cut-offs and a tee…and barefoot!

The mother was wearing no makeup, and the occasion was the daughter's wedding! The bride plopped on the couch and went to sleep!

When we arrived at what I felt was the correct dress, I applied the coral blush and lipstick and combed her blond hair. We woke the daughter in order to get her approval. She jumped up, looked at her mother and exclaimed, "Mother, you are beautiful! I've never seen you look like this!" Needless to say, I sold the dress! They had me write the makeup details down and went straight to Angie at the Lancôme Dillard's counter and bought the items I had used plus more! Even the bride had Angie do a makeup demo for her. I even had a thank-you note from the mother. This was a great learning experience for all of us!

This wedding was a prominent Dallas event, and The RoseBud was delighted to have a part in it! This family sent us several customers from Dallas.

Destination Weddings

Weddings on the beach are definitely on the marriage menu! We've done quite a few!

One bride chose a slender white lace sheath—simple but very elegant. The groom wore white trousers and an open-neck sport shirt! They chose to feel the sand between their toes, so—no shoes!

Another bride chose a filmy white chiffon dress that skimmed her body in fly-away panels.

For a ceremony in Hawaii, we dressed the mother of the groom in a gorgeous georgette ombré two-piece in shades of sunset orange. (The designer was Yolanda Lorente of Chicago.) Her accessories glittered in diamonds and gold to catch the yellow tones in the dress.

Aquamarine was the chosen color for a mother of the bride for her daughter's tropical wedding. This was a fabulous silk dress that

Rosebud Roses

caressed the body in a very flattering way. Her jewelry was blister pearls and blue topaz gemstones.

One bride and groom, in full traditional formal attire, jumped into a swimming pool to conclude their ceremony! They were both attorneys.

Another couple chose the traditional ceremony. Emily Post came in handy—it was important to get all the details right.

Weddings are happy occasions, and it feels good to be surrounded by family and friends for this special event in our lives!

Images courtesy of Athens Publishing, Inc., Waco, Texas
Sharon Wilson, Lynda Myers, Patti Thrasher,
and Michelle Clemens model fabulous fashion
for the most wonderful time of the year.

GOING TO THE WHITE HOUSE

My special friend Kitty Turner's husband, Platt Turner, was in a Houston breakfast club with George H.W. Bush, our former president. The Turners were invited to a cocktail dinner at the White House. Kitty asked me to dress her. We selected an elegant and sophisticated black coup de velour dress and accessorized with crystal and jet jewelry. We were excited!

Our state representative, Diane White Delisi, purchased a gorgeous cobalt-blue formal from The RoseBud. Her sister, Mary Alice Fifield, selected a special one-of-a-kind hand-painted georgette in charcoal ombré with hand-painted red orchids cascading over one shoulder. She also purchased a most unique silk "pineapple" cocktail bag for another outfit and had folks wanting to photograph the bag! These outfits went to the inauguration in Washington.

A customer from Killeen came in to look for a red dress to wear to the inauguration. We had the dress, and of course, it was the wrong size! I called the manufacturer and shared my desperate need for the dress in size four but—I needed it by 4:00 p.m. the next day when the customer was on her way to the inauguration in Washington. This precious gentleman sent his cutter to the factory that very night and—would you believe—we had the dress by 3:00 p.m. the next day—the right size and color!

Rosebud Roses

We even dressed Al Gore's relatives the year he was sworn in as Bill Clinton's vice president. We wished we could have dressed Hillary and Tipper—I think we could have done a better job at The RoseBud!

Through the years, we have sent many customers to Washington in RoseBud style!

From the Gatesville RoseBud, we dressed a prominent lady for the trip to Washington. Her wardrobe began with an all-over beaded formal, two silk dresses, two suits, a short red fox jacket with floppy hat to match and a gorgeous full-length tourmaline mink coat with matching hat. What a delightful experience!

I was seated with Laura Bush's first designer when I attended a Dallas Fashion Award dinner. We had a great time discussing designs and colors that would be best for her. She is such a beautiful lady and the best example of a first lady. We love the Bush family! I believe he will one day be remembered as one of our outstanding presidents of the United States. He doesn't take advice from Hollywood, and he lets the unflattering remarks and insinuations just roll off his back. He is smart and knows what he is doing. I personally have a great respect for George W. Bush!

TRUNK SHOWS

The RoseBud trunk shows brought world-famous design from Austria, Australia, England, France, Italy, Germany, Switzerland, Scotland and Canada. Dallas, Chicago, Los Angeles and New York were regular visitors. Canada brought us the world's finest custom leather designs as well as silk and linen handwoven fabrics.

Bassler's sportswear from Germany, Burberry's of London fine all-weather coats and jackets, accessories and more were finished with Helen Kaminski hats from Australia, gorgeous leather Bally bags from Switzerland and silk- or cashmere-lined leather gloves from Italy. Cashmere sweaters from Scotland and silk scarfs from all over kept the ladies very well-dressed for all occasions and destinations.

Carol Peretz's simply elegant special-occasion fashions for young and stylish mothers of the bride and groom attracted our "jet setters." Oscar de la Renta was a name that pleased fashionable ladies of all ages. I could fill hundreds of pages with the best and most sought-after labels in the industry. You name it, The RoseBud had them all.

I dressed many students for competitions in their chosen fields. We had numerous clients who found it difficult to indulge in the high-powered labels. This is where we could shine! We had something for everyone at The RoseBud, and there was no way

Rosebud Roses

we would steer one wrong. I dressed a student to compete in the law trials. Her outfit was very affordable, but she looked fantastic. She won the trials! And we were not surprised!

Fashion is a look, not a price!

Barbara Chandler, wearing Sunny Choy, demonstrates that a good suit belongs in everyone's wardrobe.

FRIENDS AT MARKET

D'Arcy has stood firm as a special friend through all the years of The RoseBud's existence. We have even visited in her New York home and had dinner with her and her husband, David. She has shared valuable information with us, leading to new and exciting adventures in the world of fashion. She even flew to our town when Altrusa presented me with a fantastic Mayor's Proclamation. She had lunch, attended the fashion show and flew back to New York, all in the same day!

Dana Melton and Paul Sutton are owners of Lori Veith Showroom at the Dallas Fashion Center. These two gentlemen are so well-versed in the business and have shared tremendous information with us in order to bring the best to The RoseBud. They are loyal friends, and we have enjoyed joining them for dinner on many occasions at market.

Jerry Brenner brought Adele Simpson fashion to The RoseBud, and we also visited with him at his showrooms in Dallas and New York. Barbara Bush was his faithful customer. Jerry invited us to dinner at his favorite restaurant in New York on several occasions. He had his own private table and special menu here. When he walked in, they rolled out the red-carpet treatment. Patti and I loved it.

Nat Ekelman had the fanciest showrooms in the Dallas

Rosebud Roses

Apparel Mart. We met Oscar de la Renta here when we shared an *Ultra* magazine ad with him. We loved Oscar's clothes, and it was rewarding to visit with him personally. He wanted to know where we found such gorgeous models, and we told him, "We grow them in our own town." He was impressed.

Helen Hsu was our favorite knit label. We sold lots of her beautiful black knit separates. Her styles were basic but beautiful and so wearable. She was a tall, attractive lady and wore her label well.

Victoria Royal was a creation of fabulous formal gowns, owned by the Sealove brothers. We were very tuned into their magnificent creations. We enlisted Melissa Mullins and Patti Thrasher as models for a couple of ads featuring this label. We sincerely like these two brilliant gentlemen.

Brad Hughes first came to the store with a strikingly beautiful line of embroidered linen separates. We placed many of these tasteful outfits in prominent wedding scenes. But, somehow, I felt that young, sun-tanned, handsome Brad, with his gorgeous prematurely silver hair, was not exactly fitted to this line of clothes.

Michael Singer introduced The RoseBud to Carol Mignon cocktail separates and dresses. We were delighted with this talented gentleman and a little in awe of him when he was associated with Christian Lacroix in Europe. (We never had this label in the store.)

Somehow Brad Hughes and Michael Singer found each other and combined their talents in the Brad Hughes and Associates Showroom in Dallas. It proved to be a positive move. The showroom is one of the largest in Fashion Dallas. Barbara, Patti and I spent lots of The RoseBud dollars here.

The Bermans, Jay and Denise, were very important to us. De Sentino was so versatile and sometimes extremely elaborate. Many times, this label was a special part of our fashion shows. We loved all the various levels of this line. When Dominique, the owner and designer of De Sentino, retired, it was like a death in The RoseBud family. And we could not talk her into staying alive in the market.

Planet was my all-time favorite and a collection of separates that actually dominated my personal closet. Lauren is a talented designer, and I am a big fan of hers. We sold lots of Planet at The RoseBud because I wore it so much. At market, store buyers would stop me in the halls and ask about what I was wearing. Black is my basic color, and Starfire Jewelry is my favorite accessory. Together, black Planet and Starfire jewels will win every time.

Yolanda Lorente stands for happy times. This magnificent collection of hand-painted silks begins on yards of pure-white luxurious silk fabric. The client chooses the design and the colors, and the story unfolds. The RoseBud sent many satisfied customers to exciting events in customized fashions. Destination weddings were popular, but sending a beautiful Yolanda creation to the White House was quite an occasion. Her lined white silk pants somehow ended up in most customers' closets because they were destined to be the beginning of a fabulous fashion statement.

BUILDING A WARDROBE IN GOOD TASTE

Good fashion never changes! Fads come and go, but good basic fashion is here to stay. A perfect wardrobe is built around a few select pieces of clothing in a basic color that is capable of presenting a variety of different looks for various occasions from morning to evening. The secret is in accessories! This is the concept on which The RoseBud was created. Customer service was our primary reason for being in business.

Fashion and style have very different meanings. Fashion is what the designers create and hope we will buy! Style reflects one's choices in what to wear. In other words, a woman of style leans toward a certain look that reflects her personality and lifestyle. So we are able to recognize her style by the clothes she wears.

As an example, I will use real people as I explain style. Both Mary Purifoy and Valerie Duncan-Callahan are tall, slender ladies with good figures. They never wear fitted designs. They prefer slim skirts or pants and tops that just skim over the body. They both lean toward classic accessories (instead of fashion jewelry). Pearls, silver, gold and diamonds are their choices. (They do own classic, fitted suits for special events.) They wear flat shoes mostly, but love heels with short skirts. They wear wide-legged pants on occasion. They love to wear linen, and they like shawls and scarfs.

Betty Thrasher

They carry large bags in good fabrics. For luncheons, dinners and formal occasions, small purses are preferred.

Katherine Myers is a small, petite size and leans toward fitted garments. She has the figure to wear this style. For casual wear, you'll see her in attractive cotton pants, tops, jackets and good-looking tennis shoes. But when she dresses for a special evening out, she is simply gorgeous and tastefully attired.

Barbara Chandler loves the latest fashion has to offer! This is probably why we chose to use her in so many RoseBud ads. She is a beautiful blonde who always wanted to be a redhead. If it is glamour we're searching for, Barbara is our girl! She is such fun! She, Patti and I had some exciting times together, and we are all as different as night and day—yet so much alike. And we span such different ages.

Patti Thrasher prefers that "girl next door" look. Her choice in fashion is personally low key. However, she is so naturally beautiful that everything looks good on her. Her blond hair and olive complexion are a great asset. She possesses the height that allows her to wear great-looking flat shoes. She leans toward big handbags. The RoseBud coaxed her into modeling for more *Ultra* magazine ads than she was comfortable with. I am so fortunate to claim her as my daughter-in-law!

Sharla Winkler has modeled for me for many years. We can put anything on Sharla, and it looks fabulous! She is wonderful to work with, and in real life, she is an executive assistant to the president of Baylor Scott & White Central Texas Foundation. Sharla prefers simple designs with less flair. She is a tall brunette who is able to maintain her perfect size-ten figure. We would say that she likes fitted, tailored garments.

Marcine Chambers holds an impressive position in the Foundation office at Scott & White Hospital. She is full-figured and loves color. However, we see her wearing lots of black and brown. She has been a regular on my runways. Marcine tends to like conservative accessories unless she is attending some festive events for the hospital. And then she might indulge in a little glitz.

Jessica Walker, the mother of three boys, is very involved in their various activities. She can hold her own in athletic work-out clothes or the fanciest formal attire. She has a great, toned figure, a contagious smile and beautiful, long brown hair.

Ann Secrest is an elegant lady, and classic design is her forte. She's a size 4/6 with salt-and-pepper hair, a beautiful woman who is striking on the runway. You want everything she wears because she does such a beautiful job of modeling. Her husband and her son are both attorneys.

So here we have examples of a variety of fashion looks. Each one is to be admired. What is your style?

Personally, for me, at the age of eighty-something, I don't want to look like an old, tired woman, nor do I desire to wear the clothes of a twenty-year-old. My style is absolutely mine alone. With my white hair and olive complexion, I feel best in black. I wear lots of pants, slim-legged or wide-legged. I do not wear anything fitted, but I like easy tunics with long sleeves that I can push up and necklines that prove to be a great background for jewelry.

I wear Starfire Designs by Charlie Wharton every day, without question! My jewelry is complementary to sweats, jogging suits, day wear, casuals or the most formal affairs. I am never without my jewelry. My favorites are a pyrite cluster on a gold neckwire, an embossed gold and silver cuff (bracelet), square mother-of-pearl ear clips and ring (especially made for me by Lazaro in New York).

I do have a special diamond ring, inherited from my Aunt Rose, that I am never without. It will be passed on to Patti.

GENERAL ADVICE

When I read Stanley Marcus's book, *Minding the Store*, I was surprised that my feelings about the retail clothing business were so closely related to his thoughts. I did not know Mr. Marcus at the time, but many years later, when I had my own store, The RoseBud, I had the pleasure of meeting him.

Our philosophy at The RoseBud was so similar to that of the Neiman Marcus family. Neiman's was, without a question, the most successful and well-known retail clothing business in America. The main purpose of the store was to be in tune to each customer's preferences of style, color, size, fit and lifestyle. This requires substantial homework. I was taught at an early age to put customers' faces into garments when on buying trips to market. I was never known to put personal needs and wants before my customer. No matter how much I was attracted to an item of clothing, the customer had the first choice. When a special garment or outfit was purchased by a client, it was absolutely off-limits to ourselves and our associates. There was one lone incident when a sales associate was regrettably allowed to order a special outfit that had been sold to a very good, loyal, local customer. The associate promised to never, ever wear this outfit except when out of town! I believed that she could be trusted to uphold our agreement. Lo and behold, both ladies showed up at the local country club in the identical ensemble. This was a lesson hard-learned. Never again would I make such a mistake!

Confidentiality is an important practice in a store like The RoseBud. Who bought what is not on the agenda—ever! But many times we were selling items that were purchased in several different sizes and colors. When we sold one in a particular area and later had a customer who wanted that same dress, we would declare that it had already been sold in her town and we would prefer that she select another great style. On one occasion we had three very close friends who wanted to buy the same dress but in different colors. This was a special circumstance, so we honored their request, but this particular style was never sold again to another person in that town.

Sportswear was a very different story, in that an outfit was made up of several different pieces, and it was rare if two ladies came out looking exactly alike. Each person has her own style, and different pieces in a sportswear collection will (most times) result in very different outfits. Accessories make a huge impact, and two ladies may select the exact two or three styles from a designated separates group and emerge with totally different looks. The magic is always in how one puts the total look together.

Some folks have a built-in talent for creating dynamic results in fashion. Others have very different talents. This is what makes the fashion industry so exciting! Do your own thing if this makes you happy. If you are unsure about putting a look together, by all means, shop with a store that will give you the assistance you need. There is talent out there. All you must do is look around until you find that particular sales associate that is able to fill your needs and produce the results that will bring you the most comfort and satisfaction.

The best advice I can share is to always place quality over quantity. It is much smarter to build a fashion foundation with a basic color (I like black), quality fabric and design that best fits your lifestyle. Stick to plain old common sense and select the most flattering styles to enhance your personal body shape. (Every woman was not created to wear the latest gimmicks on the runways or in the magazines. Get real!)

Choose fabulous, all-around basic accessories that will serve you well. Be sure to have a good leather bag for all times, a smart small purse for luncheons and dinner…and please wear good shoes that are kept in perfect repair! Good skin care is a must! A great haircut always looks good, and manicures are a real plus!

HANDBAGS AND PURSES

For daytime, ladies prefer a bag large enough to handle everyday needs—and then some. We usually only change out these bags for various seasons. The fabric should be very durable. The color should be basic. For those who do change bags occasionally, the fabric will depend on lifestyle. For the lady professional, a good leather bag is recommended in her basic color choice.

For luncheons and dinners, it is wise to choose a small purse—just large enough to carry the essentials like lipstick, driver's license, credit card or cash and tissue. Do not let this purse become stuffed. If more room is needed, move up to a slightly larger size. Huge bags are in poor taste.

For formal events, select a small, elegant purse in good taste to complement the outfit being worn. Large bags are out of the question!

For all-around occasions, a smart leather bag in a size that fits the wearer is best. Keep it tasteful. Your handbag says a lot about you!

THE BASIC WARDROBE

The perfect basic wardrobe would most likely contain the following items in the color black, plus a couple of white pieces:

CLOTHING

Slim pant
Full-legged pant
Cropped pant
Long skirt (slim or flared)
Short, straight skirt (only for great legs)
Sleeveless shell (white)
Sleeveless shell (black)
Black cocktail dress
Fitted jacket
Unfitted jacket
Crisp white cotton shirt
Sweater (pullover)
White silk blouse
Sweater (cardigan)
Pair of good jeans
Rain or all-weather coat
Walking shorts
Two or three colorful scarfs
One good shawl

Accessories

Black pumps (heels)
Colored flats
Black boots
Tennis shoes
Black sandals (heels)
Black flats
High-heeled gold or silver sandals
Big black leather bag
Small black silk purse
Jewelry: gold, silver, pearl

It is perfectly natural to collect these suggested wardrobe items as time goes by. We may not be able to have all these pieces at the beginning. The moral to this story is to shop wisely. Put some serious thought into purchases. Once you own all the pieces, you are set for life! But—be sure to replace items that show their age. Most importantly, choose good quality over quantity every time. It is always better to have the best rather than the less expensive. Quality will last longer.

A good hat is wise if you live in an area of extreme weather conditions. Gloves are important, too. I love my leather gloves lined in silk or cashmere.

The interior of The RoseBud in Temple.

IT'S IN THE CLOSET

I always thought about how much fun it would be to get into ladies' closets and show them the treasures that hang there unnoticed! Little separate pieces may come together to create a masterpiece. Through time, we collect value that is easy to overlook, especially if we are not trained to see the full potential of every separate piece.

For example, I have had lined white silk pants by Yolanda Lorente for many years. I have taken special care of them. (Only Eddie at Pittman's Cleaners has been trusted to clean them.) These trousers are trained to take on a multitude of tops in various fabrics. Refined cottons, real linens, lush velvets, laces and silks, as well as fine woolens and cashmeres, have transformed these trousers into fabulous outfits. And just think, only one pair of white silk pants brought this magic to my closet!

Accessories also do magic tricks! But, even here in this category, basics have an important place. It takes great footwear—flats, heels, sandals, pumps, boots, glitz—to pull off the perfect look. Handbags and purses have a definite impact on a great look. The big guy in the picture is our jewelry! Great thought must go into the basic pieces—gold, pearl and silver. Precious and semiprecious stones are most likely the icing on the cake. All of these suggestions are ideal. We may not be able to collect all the pieces for the puzzle. But this is something to work toward for the

Betty Thrasher

best results. The bottom line is to choose quality over quantity and keep the basic pieces in good repair.

I am very pleased with the jewelry I have collected over the years. I wear my gold Starfire neckwire every day! I have several interchangeable pendants to add to the neckpiece. My favorite is the pyrite cluster. People comment on this necklace every day—the checker at Sam's or HEB as well as the banker, world traveler or socialite. We all have an eye for beautiful things! At the same time, I can wear my most valuable piece, and no one will comment.

Dress by: Victoria Royal • Location: Residence of Judge and Mrs. Jack Prescott.

The finest in special occasion dressing...

Monday - Saturday...10 - 6
(appointments honored)

Exchange Plaza, Loop 363   Temple, Texas   (817)774-1978

Victoria Royal was famous for special occasion attire, as worn here by Patti Thrasher.

FASHION LABELS

The RoseBud was proud to offer the finest labels in the world of fashion. We were delighted to bring to our customers names like Bassler of Germany, Geiger of Austria, Burberry of England, Kaminski from Australia, Bally from Switzerland, Zonda Nellis and Lyn Leather from Canada, beautiful cashmeres from Scotland, many silk labels from France and Italy and much more. Our handbag and purse names were the very best in the world, and we placed great significance on accessories.

In the early days, labels like Jerry Silverman (ultrasuedes), Susie Hayward, Mary Ann Restivo, Agatha Brown, Vittadini, Paul Stanley, Joan Vass, Zanella, Escada, Dana Buchman, Hino and Mallee, Ellen Tracy, Ann Pinkerton, Mondi and Zelda were at the top of our list.

Knits were easy for travel, and The RoseBud had the crème of the crop in Helen Hsu (our favorite), Richlee, Almoral, Forté and St. John. Knits were comfortable, packable and very basic. Sportswear was very important, allowing ladies to select a few basic pieces upon which to build a wardrobe.

Coats and shawls, as well as capes and jackets, were essential. For the all-around practical need, we loved Mycra Pac all-weather jackets and coats in a variety of lengths. Adrienne Landau's fabulous capes were very appealing. Fleurette coats in cashmere and fine fabrics were trimmed with elegant furs. Lyn Leather jackets and pants took us everywhere in those luscious custom-made creations. Last, but certainly not least, were the great all-weather Burberry coats in smart basic colors with zip-out liners.

The Jane Yoo handbag line was practical, beautiful and extremely popular among our ladies. A customer could never be satisfied with just one! Billfolds, coin purses, checkbook covers, credit card holders, etc. were also available. There were many designs to choose from, too. Belts were also popular. These items would last a lifetime!

Hats were so much fun! Some were for flair; some were necessary (like Helen Kaminiski) and could be packed for travel without disturbing the shape. Some like St. John, Frank Olive and Eric Javitz were serious while Kokin hats, as outlandish as they seemed, were like icing on a cake! Carol Carr, J.R. Ross and Shady Brady were best for western affairs.

Our jewels sparkled from all directions. We loved Patrice (bugs, frogs and beetles in their best colors and metals). Lee Wolfe's strictly clean-lined gold and silver pieces were starkly practical. R.J. Goraziano and Monies featured conversation pieces that were brave and bold. Kenneth Jay Lane copied those very expensive brooches and necklaces that only the very wealthy could own. (He told me that Barbara Bush ordered her fake pearls from him.) Swarovski jewelry was elegant and noticeable, and the quality was superb. One gentleman who purchased a crystal necklace for his wife referred to it as her diamond piece. Diane Malouf had its very own look—very smart! Susan Green's collection featured antique beads and chains while it was kind of custom made (I loved it). Lordane was everything one could imagine in costume jewelry! You name it, Lordane had it! Whiting and Davis was known for its gold and silver mesh items. Maya was heavy on the jewels with purses, earrings and bracelets—very appealing.

Accessories will either make or break an outfit! This is the finishing touch and will reflect one's personality. This is the fun part of getting dressed!

A closet of good quality black separates in a year-round fabric will take us anywhere! The jewelry, handbag or purse and the shoes will dictate the direction we wish to take.

Jewelry needed:

Pearls (two lengths)
Silver neck or chain
Gold neck or chain
Crystal earrings
(ears to match necks)

These items will go everywhere, anytime! Good taste is imperative, and good fashion never goes out of style. Fads and trends come and go.

The best investment is to take the time to shop wisely. Never shop hurriedly! Think before acting. Find a salesperson who is knowledgeable and won't steer you wrong. She should be trustworthy and have your best interests at heart. This person is out there. Sometimes, we must search to find her.

OUR BEST ACCESSORIES

Natural, well-applied makeup and clean, shiny hair are our very best accessories. This is the beginning of our well-dressed appearance.

A smart hairstylist will suggest a good haircut in order to achieve that special personal look that sets us apart from others. This is the beginning of our personal style. (Please—no weird styling or wild colors!) Natural, healthy hair has a clean sheen. Color is sometimes helpful and exciting, but be sure your stylist is reputable and knows that "natural" is the name of the game. (I believe He really knew what He was doing when God, the top stylist, colored our hair!) It is okay to enhance our color, but to think pink, orange or maroon is attractive tells a lot about the person. Our hair is our "crown and glory"! A good thought to remember.

Makeup says a lot about us! It is so important to keep it clean and natural. Radiant skin tones may need toning down. Pale skin might call for a little color boost. Neutral is key! Makeup is certainly necessary because it protects the skin from the elements. Failing to protect our skin may lead to premature aging or blemishes. Proper cleansing is a must! Never go to bed without cleansing your face. I use a cleanser plus Dove soap and water.

We have prepared our spotless canvas by removing all traces of makeup. Now we can begin to put the painting on the canvas.

Rosebud Roses

1. Moisturize. Smooth a thin application over the entire face and throat.
2. Apply a light film of makeup base over the entire face. (Do not put makeup on the neck!) If more coverage is needed, apply another slight coat of base in those areas, keeping it clean and simple.
3. Apply a light dusting of translucent powder over the face with a clean brush.
4. Brush the brows up and out. Lightly fill in with brow pencil or brush. Match the hair if possible. For very blonde or white-silver hair, taupe pencil is best. Never tweeze above the brow! Only tweeze hairs below the natural line of the brow. (Thin brows are not pretty!)
5. Paint the entire eyelid with an ivory shadow. Lightly brush brown shadow through the center of the lid in order to create an indention and to take away any puffiness.
6. Line the eyes softly. The purpose of lining is to help the lashes look thicker. Black lines can be very harsh. (We do not want to look like a raccoon.) Brown liner is best for most, but colored liner may be quite nice for some occasions.
7. Black mascara is good for most of us when it is properly applied. (Avoid thick, clumpy lashes.)
8. For cheeks and lips, my choice is coral because it is a healthy, natural color that complements all of fashion's clothing colors. Natural is the key!
9. Garish colors are trends that come and go, never to come across as serious. Natural, clean makeup will always be acceptable. Natural is here to stay!

Our hair and makeup are our most important accessories. When this is right, very little else matters! So keep your face pretty! This is how we will be remembered.

SHOES

Shoes can work miracles! They must be taken seriously and kept in good condition! They *do* make a difference!

Sandals are mostly worn without hose, only when the feet are in good condition! Hosiery (sheer toe and heel *only*) are suggested for very special occasions! Color should be kept light and very sheer! (I prefer pearl polish for toes because it goes with everything!)

Closed-toe heels or peep-toe shoes require hosiery (only sheer toe)! Pumps are the perfect shoes for professional business! Summer calls for light, sheer hose, while for winter, opt for sheer or opaque black with black shoes! I have always liked sheer ivory hose with black shoes when wearing pearls!

Silver, gold, bronze and pewter shoes are handsome with cocktail and formal wear! Colors add excitement to the outfit but must be right! No guessing!

Flats and tennis are musts for the very casual occasions!

LET'S FACE IT

Having spent more than forty years in the skin care business, I was shocked to discover that women took their personal skin care regimen so lightly. My company, Beauty Counselor, had the very best cosmetic chemist in the country. Ed de Navarre lived in Grosse Point, Michigan, when he developed a product he called Fountain of Beauty, a very rich, creamy-textured product that produced positive results. His skin care products were 99.9 percent pure, and it was clearly easy to spot the ladies who followed suggestions and used these products on a regular basis. There was no magic trick, just common sense and pure products.

This skin care company believed that well-groomed, well-educated ladies could go into a client's home and teach proper skin care on a one-on-one basis. These representatives were called Beauty Counselors. They attended weekly training sessions under the eagle eye of special instructors. I was one of these instructors, and I was extremely proud of my loyal clientele!

No makeup products will perform well if we have not taken the necessary steps to prepare the facial skin. This is a fact! I have had ladies tell me that they have never worn makeup, but what they are really saying is "I don't take care of my skin." This absolutely floors me! Makeup actually serves to protect the skin from the elements.

THE PINK SPORTSWEAR

I have a great story about an incident shared with the "Three Musketeers" (Louise, Frances and me). While at market, I placed a very important order for a group of pink sportswear separates. When it was about time to receive the order, we had a call informing us that the merchandise was not available in pink but could be substituted in navy blue. (Freda Hanks had requested an outfit in pink.) I gave the company permission to send the navy group.

Frances and Louise were working that day, and I was in the office, expressing my disappointment in learning that the group was not available in pink. Frances said, "Okay, ladies, join hands. We are going to ask God to come to the rescue." As Frances spoke her prayer, she said, "God, just send the angels out to gather our pink sportswear group! Betty really needs this, especially for Freda." I could not keep from laughing as I visualized these precious angels flitting around gathering pink separates.

And then there was a knock on the door! Our stockroom manager, Sandy, was standing there with a very shocked look on her beautiful face as she said, "You are not going to believe this, but that navy-blue sportswear group is here, and it is *not* navy blue! It is pink!" We all nearly lost our breath. Moral to this story: never question what God can do!

THE KENTUCKY DERBY

The RoseBud dressed quite a few ladies for the Kentucky Derby. One trip to market still stands out in my mind. We were always searching for fabulous hats. The most fabulous hat for all times was staring me in the face! I had never seen a more impressive hat and of course, it was terribly expensive for a spring chapeau! I tried to walk away from this gorgeous creation, but it just kept calling me back! So—I bought it! My reasoning was that if it didn't sell, I could always use it on our mannequins in window displays.

The day "the hat" arrived, we proudly placed it on display. It had not been the center of attraction for more than a few minutes when a customer we had never seen before walked into The RoseBud and went straight to "the hat"! She bought this phenomenal creation! My intuition had paid off. In my heart, I knew there was a lady out there that would absolutely love wearing this most gorgeous hat at the Kentucky Derby!

Shelley had grown up in the traditions of Churchill Downs. We had to coax her to share stories about this famous event! We asked her to wear her personal Derby outfit in our "Legends of Fashion" show benefitting McLane Children's Hospital. She was beautiful!

ROSEBUD STAFF

Willie Mae Harrison

Willie Mae Harrison was the first employee at The RoseBud in Temple. She was in the lingerie department at Dyers Department Store. Willie was a beautiful, petite blonde with a flawless ivory complexion who wore her fashionable clothes well. When Charlene and I saw her, we knew that she would be perfect at The RoseBud in Temple. We made an appointment to have lunch with Willie. I was a little under the weather that day, so Charlene and Willie had a good visit, and Charlene hired Willie to work at The RoseBud.

Willie developed quite a clientele and served them well. She was with us for sixteen years before she moved to Dallas.

Louise Chipman

Louise Chipman was a faith-filled Christian and quite an inspiration to me. She grew up in the beauty of Bandera, Texas, and attended the University of Texas at Austin. She was a member of Delta Zeta Sorority.

Louise loved fashion, arriving for work at The RoseBud wearing beautifully coordinated outfits, complete with matching accessories, hats and shoes. We looked forward to seeing what she would be wearing each day. She always said, "God likes for us to look good." But she would be the first to say that God loves all of us, regardless of how we are dressed.

Louise's handwriting was outstanding, and because of this special talent, she was placed in charge of all our mail-outs. She hand-addressed thousands of our newsletters, Rose Petals. The pretty pale-pink linen envelopes with Louise's special touch went out to our customers on a regular schedule, keeping them properly informed of news in the world of fashion at The RoseBud! She even searched post offices for postage stamps with a rose. When she located the perfect one, she would buy all the stamps that were available. Our mail list grew at a rapid pace, so Louise engaged her friend, Frances Madeley, to help. These two ladies were the perfect ones to see that all RoseBud correspondence went out in grand style. They were also great backstage on fashion show days. All of us at The RoseBud valued these ladies.

When Louise went to heaven, she left a great void in my life, but all of us will forever cherish her memory.

Cynthia Newton is Louise Chipman's daughter. Her children, Celeste and Maxwell are very dear to us. In fact, Maxwell is our godson. We have celebrated Christmas Eve together for many years! Cindy is a CPA by trade and is a very busy lady. Celeste has followed in her mother's footsteps and is employed with a prominent firm in Dallas. Maxwell is currently a student at UT in Austin.

MARY BRYAN PURIFOY

Mary Purifoy is a cool lady. The first time I ever saw her, Ann Chamlee brought her to The RoseBud in Gatesville, Texas. She was very striking, and it was hard not to stare. She is tall, slender and has beautifully shaped legs. Her gorgeous short curly hair is snow white. She definitely has a style all her own. Black and white are her favorite colors, and they dominate her closet. She favors long wide-legged trousers and simple loose-fitting tunics, even though she has the perfect figure. She wears flat, casual shoes unless she chooses a short black skirt—this is when the elegant black high heels appear on the scene. Her jewelry is pearl, silver, gold or diamond, but always tasteful, never flashy!

Mary's makeup is clean and natural, never overdone except when we insist for the fashion shows. She will always be remembered as a runway favorite. When she is complimented, she will insist on pitching the kind and flattering words right back to the giver. She can cry at the drop of a hat.

Mary and husband Al had three children. Johnny is a pilot with American Airlines. His wife, Kim, was also with American as a flight attendant. They live in Dallas. Sally and her husband, Scott Crowe, have two children, Kate and Caleb, who attend Texas Christian University in Fort Worth. The Crowes make their home in Dallas. Mack followed his dad into the Purifoy Insurance Company in Temple. He is a very popular young man. All the Purifoys are attractive and well-liked.

Al has passed away, and Mary has downsized and moved to the Meridian Retirement Center, where she makes folks feel right at home. Mary has always been a "people person."

BARBARA CHANDLER

I first met Barbara during the hippie era. She had two darling children when she married Dr. Jim Chandler. They were perfect together! I loved their little family.

Barbara was tall and slender with a perfect size eight figure. I could visualize her on my runway. So I approached her about working part-time at the store. This appealed to her and she accepted the job. My intuition paid off! She could wear anything and make it look good! She was a knockout on The RoseBud runways!

Barbara was a quick study. She became seriously interested in the world of fashion and soon cultivated a loyal clientele. Ladies took her fashion advice to heart. She was fun to work with, so Patti

Rosebud Roses

and I decided to invite her to make market trips with us. She was soon a natural in this capacity. Shortly after, we began making two trips to the New York markets each year.

Barbara grew up in England. Her parents came to New York to celebrate Christmas each year, so she became familiar with this magic city. The family moved to America when Barbara was sixteen.

When we decided it was necessary to make buying trips to New York, Patti and I asked Barbara to join us. The three of us made a great team! Each of us had her own personal style, which was a great asset to our buying trips. We each had a good "eye" for recognizing quality, design and style! We could cover all the bases from three very different perspectives. These trips were fun and exciting with our RoseBud customers in mind.

We cultivated some valuable friends in New York and beyond. Many outstanding vendors came to New York from various countries. We had good friends from all over the world, and quite a few of them visited The RoseBud in Temple, Texas!

These were exciting times when The RoseBud was known for the outstanding fashion we were bringing to Central Texas. I am proud to say that Barbara was delightful to have on our buying staff. She was always searching for new and interesting features and ideas. She had a good eye for construction and color. She was always ready to dive into new ideas and make them work for her customers, who were very loyal to her. She developed a huge following, and ladies of all ages trusted her judgment.

Barbara Chandler was a wonderful gift. She had no idea that she was such a natural beauty. She was absolutely striking on our runways, and I loved using Barbara in our ads. We chose her to model in one of our most effective *Ultra* magazine ads, wearing a Mary Ann Sinclair creation, photographed with Inez Arnold's Excalibur automobile in the circular drive of a beautiful brick home in the Canyon Creek area of Temple.

Barbara and Jim opened their home to the staff and models of The RoseBud for special events. We all felt very much at home in the presence of Barbara and Jim Chandler. Jim Chandler was a genius and a real credit to Scott & White Hospital—we all adored him. Jim passed away and left a huge void in our lives. He was well-loved by his patients and friends. The Chandlers will always have a special place in the hearts of those who were blessed to call them friends.

PATTI THRASHER

Patti was a real bonus when she joined our RoseBud staff! She was gorgeous "clear to the bone," and we all felt so blessed to have her on our team! I could just imagine her working with our customers and dominating the RoseBud runways! She would have no part of my plan.

Patti was a blessing in the office. She was one to seriously attend to business, and this was no bad trait in our store! She kept us all on our toes—but in a very nice way! (I felt it was a shame to hide all that beauty in the office where she seldom would be seen.)

It took some tall-talking, but we did convince her to be the subject of our first *Ultra* magazine ad! She was beautiful! This was a spring ad filmed in Austin's Zilker Park on one of the coldest days in November! She never flinched! The ad was perfectly gorgeous. The subject was an Oscar de la Renta two-piece cocktail outfit. It was a popular ad with customers. We sold several, in different areas of Texas. The last request for this dress came from a lady in New York City.

ANN CHAMLEE

Ann was a master pianist and, without a doubt, the best of the best at the piano. We all looked to her with tremendous admiration! One never had to wonder what was on her mind! Ann had a heart as big as the world and always stood ready to help folks in need. She was a unique personality. She was always ready to serve her Temple.

The town was very important to her, and her all-time goal was to give the best of her tremendous God-given talent to her city!

The Temple Civic Theatre held her in high esteem, and she was in her natural element here.

Martha Jean Burleson

Martha Jean Burleson was a welcomed addition to our RoseBud staff. She was one of the elite Northside Ladies, and they loved having Martha Jean at the RoseBud!

Martha Jean and Lloyd Burleson had five beautiful daughters. Each one was extremely attractive in her own way. Martha Jean grew up in a prominent family in St. Joseph, Missouri. She was the most loved lady by folks of all ages. Our precious friend passed away very unexpectedly just before Christmas 2014. We miss her terribly.

Customers at The RoseBud adored this special lady! I never knew her to be in a bad mood. She only saw the world through rose-colored glasses!

Priscilla Hill

Priscilla was a colorful character who seemed to identify with people. She was very good at displays and floral arrangements. When fashion show time came, Priscilla could get the job done. She was an incredibly hard worker.

Part-time Employees

Many young folks have been a vital part of The RoseBud in Temple. We cherished the brief times they were with us!

Hope Carberry, Whitney King, Sarah Arnold, Brittany Elkins, Wendy Wilson, Sherri Sebastian, Lynda Myers, Gina Weiner, Ann Chamlee, Michelle Clemens, Jean Gosney, Jennifer Popple, Lanelle Fikes, Mattie Ingram, Margie Sanchez, Sandy McMurtry, Moni Bittenbinder, Valerie Duncan, Liz Popejoy, Rendan Harper, Sharon

Childers, Anna Kauppila and Cat Landry passed through The RoseBud on their way to other projects or commitments.

Elsie Carlson, Mildred Bruggman, Marta and Lillie Kelly were our dedicated seamstresses until Elsie Springer came to stay.

I can honestly say that each one of these special people were an asset to our store—The RoseBud! We will always be grateful for the time they spent with us!

Front Row: Mary, Katherine and Sharon;
Back row: Martha Jean and Ann.

BILL HORTON

After we were established and going full-swing in the Temple RoseBud, a well-dressed gentleman with an impressive attaché case came calling. His name was William G. Horton, and he was from Dallas. He specialized in professional displays at outstanding prestigious boutiques and department stores. He shared photos of exciting displays in stores like Neiman Marcus, Gucci, Chanel and even Trump Tower in New York. So, needless to say, we jumped on the bandwagon, and soon Bill and his talented team were creating seasonal displays at The RoseBud!

We became very good friends, so when the Visionaries staged "Legends of Fashion" to benefit the new Scott & White McLane Children's Hospital in Temple, Bill drove into our town in his big panel truck filled with exquisite props and exotic fresh flowers to create four smashing window displays.

The foyer of the Frank W. Mayborn Convention Center came to life with the elegance of the most elite fashion boutique! Each of the displays featured one of the four seasons of the year.

Bill Horton's displays: Spring, Summer, Fall and Winter.

THE BIG HEART ATTACK

New Year's Eve brought the surprise of my life! To end 2006 with a huge heart attack was certainly not on my agenda.

We were leaving Dr. Gary Gosney's Chinese mansion after a successful fundraiser for the Temple Civic Theatre. As I opened the car door, I felt the sharpest, most tremendous pain across my chest! I told Bob, "I have pulled a muscle across by chest, and it hurts like nothing I have ever felt!" I drove us home, clear across town, and settled into a chair in our living room. The excruciating pain would not leave! Bob called 911.

Have you ever been in the presence of one who knew death was certain? This is how I felt. I knew that I was going to die! I told Bob, "You better call 911 again because I am not going to make it."

At that moment, the EMT rushed through the door! Evidently, these people really know what that are doing. Before I knew it, there was an IV in my arm, and I was on a gurney headed for an ambulance. The last thing I remember is a young man saying, "Mrs. Thrasher, we are taking good care of you."

I do not remember arriving at Scott & White emergency room. I do not recall the cath lab. On New Year's Day, I had open-heart surgery for five bypasses! I was in ICU for a short time after surgery. My daughter-in-law saw me being placed in a wheelchair, headed for a hospital patient room. This was not going to happen.

Patti suggested that I be returned to ICU immediately! I ended up staying in ICU for two weeks. Twice I almost did not make it!

I asked for paper and pen because I could not speak. I was very frightened. My grandson, Jeff, was in ICU with me. The nurse said that I could not have the paper and pen. Jeff came to my rescue and told the nurse, "She can have anything she wants!" I still have the notes I attempted to scribble, begging not to be left alone. This was the most traumatic time in my life!

I will always remember how diligent my family was, especially my son, Dr. Michael Thrasher. He called a special meeting with doctors and family. I am told that fourteen people were present. This probably saved my life, and I will always be grateful for this special attention to my needs.

One incident stands out clearly in my hazy memory. I was in a hospital bed. The room was rather dark, and several people were standing around my bed. I only saw one face: my brother, Tom Tapman! I felt a tear roll down my cheek and fell asleep. The room was very peaceful.

It took nearly seven months for me to feel decent again. A great depression came over me, and I wondered if I'd ever be me, Betty Thrasher, again! In the meantime, it was decided that it was time for The RoseBud to be sold. (It broke my heart!) Daughter-in-law Patti came to the rescue and attended to the sale of the store.

Bob and Betty at Dr. Gary Gosney's Chinese mansion the night of Betty's heart attack.

THE SALE OF THE ROSEBUD

Sherri Davis had expressed a desire to own The RoseBud. She was a close friend, like one of my children. Patti approached her, and she said that she was interested in the purchase of the store. I was pleased to pass the good reputation of The RoseBud to one that I felt had the passion and financial means to carry on the success of The RoseBud. The sale of the store was completed on the seventeenth of May 2007.

The new owners asked me and Patti to stay on staff as advisers, and I was also requested to help stage the fashion shows and attend market with the new owners. After the Altrusa show in November, I was busy returning merchandise to stock and revamping the showroom. At the end of the day, I was leaving the store when the new owner called me back to the sidewalk and handed me a letter relieving me of any and all association with The RoseBud!

It was the end of a beautiful experience in the world of fashion, I thought! But soon other stores were needing my help, and I have been very busy ever since. However, nothing could ever measure up to the wonderful years in my fabulous store, The RoseBud.

I am sorry that The RoseBud could not live on for many years longer. The Davises decided to close the store. The RoseBud will always be missed by our loyal customers—and me! The RoseBud was not "work" to me. It was a joy! I am so blessed to have had the privilege of being able to live my dream.

And YES! I would do it all over again!

STARFIRE DESIGNS BY CHARLIE WHARTON

When Charlie Wharton came to The RoseBud, his mission was to convince me to have a trunk show. I was very impressed with his fabulous collection of precious and semiprecious gemstones from around the world. The designs were spectacular and, twenty years later, my thoughts and feelings about Starfire are unchanged.

After I sold The RoseBud and the new owners closed the store, Charlie and I still worked together as a team to promote and offer the outstanding popularity of Starfire Designs. We have always been partners.

Charlie has always been the definite designer of his gorgeous jewels, but his wife, Jean, is extremely talented in her own right, and together, they make a great team.

Charlie has the absolute solution for that perfect gift. Who wouldn't love a sparkling Starfire gemstone pendent, ring, bracelet or earrings under the Christmas tree? Gentlemen: those coffee pots and vacuum cleaners just don't cut it. Ladies: wear it Christmas morning! Starfire jewels are just great with pajamas!

Birthdays and anniversaries or special events are perfect occasions for giving a thoughtful gift to someone special—wife, daughter, mom, sister or friend.

Betty Thrasher

Charlie and I enjoy staging Starfire trunk shows around the country. We love having our friends lend a helping hand assisting clients in making the right choice. I wear Starfire every day. It is the finished asset to an outfit. I love it!

TO SET THE RECORD STRAIGHT

The RoseBud was never an "on-sale discount store." We prided ourselves in offering the best quality merchandise at the best price for our customers. We only concentrated on two sales each year at the end of the major seasons—Spring and Fall! If I still had my store today, this would be enforced. The RoseBud's reputation was based on good, sincere service and merchandise, not on sales!

I have a wonderful Mycra Pac all-weather reversible full-length raincoat. Everyone wanted the coat, so I stopped by the showroom one day and learned the coat had been discontinued. The manufacturer said, "No one dresses up anymore!"

I was in shock! I never, ever thought I had to be dressed-up to wear this fabulous, versatile coat. So I said to her, "We did not receive this news in Texas. I guess I will need to tell ladies not to dress up anymore!" I wear this coat with sweats and tennis shoes as well as my best outfit. And I could stand on a street corner all day long and sell as many of these coats as the owner could manufacture.

I wore the coat in Dallas North Park Mall one day when it was raining. My friend, Valerie Callahan, was with me. We had so many ladies stop and ask where they could buy this coat that Val said, "Take that coat off! We'll never get anything done as long as folks can see that coat!" And, I might add, we never had a Mycra Pac coat on sale. The secret is knowing what will attract one's clientele.

I think all manufacturers of women's clothes should be required to spend time on the sales floor and in dressing rooms. This is where we find the secret to selecting the correct merchandise for the folks we are serving.

Service was our primary reason for being in business. Our attention was directed to the needs of our customers. We really never paid attention to the operation of other stores.

Popular-priced merchandise is more likely to be found in department store chains, where discounts are common practice. The RoseBud never concentrated on discounts, but our mission was to bring the finest quality at the best possible prices to our customers. We had two seasonable sales each year but were never "on sale" twelve months of the year. The RoseBud was never intended to be a discount store. We had much respect for our clients and took good care of our stock, which was always first class.

We did our job well, always with our customers' needs above all else. We all felt very positive about our wonderful years at The RoseBud until the sale of the store in 2007. That was a very sad day for me.

THE ROSEBUD AWNING

After Sherri's The RoseBud closed its doors, a worker at the building found the impressive green awning that had hung above the entrance to the store in the dumpster. He realized that his discovery was valuable, so he retrieved it from the dumpster and loaded it into the bed of his pickup truck. He drove to Veranda Bloom, a beautiful antique store in Rogers, Texas. He asked his friends Regina and Marcia if they would like to have it.

The ladies were delighted and said to the man, Andres Gonzalez, "Oh yes, we would love to have this awning. It belonged to our friend, Betty Thrasher, the original owner of The RoseBud in Temple." This mother-daughter team, originally from Gatesville, cleaned the awning and proudly hung it in their shop.

When I heard this story, it brought a torrent of tears to my eyes! My beautiful awning that I had cherished so was now in the hands of precious friends, who were very aware of its great importance.

A special thanks to Andres Gonzales for preserving my dream.

A LESSON IN GIVING

It is important to me that my readers know and understand how The RoseBud became a reality.

This is not one's usual reason for venturing into a business. I never really gave much thought to how much money I could make. It was much more important to put the emphasis on how good I could make customers feel when shopping for clothes. I believe with all my heart that when we look good, we feel good. When we feel good, it is so easy to greet the world around us with a positive attitude and a great smile! Happy folks are fun to be around.

The first lesson was a hard one. I was just a little girl when a couple came into Dad's store, Harry's Place, with their little girl. It was a cold day, and the little girl had no shoes and no warm clothes. My dad looked at me and said, "Betty, get your beautiful pink Roman sandals and matching silk socks and a warm sweater. We'll give these things to this little girl." It was amazing how this made me feel. These were my favorite shoes! But the little girl needed them more than I did.

Tears welled up in my eyes. Dad waited to see what I would do. My heart won the battle, and I gave my dearest possession to someone less fortunate. This was a tremendous lesson and one I shall never forget. I felt so warm inside. And I will never forget my dad for this lesson in life.

Betty wearing the pink roman sandals that
Daddy asked her to give away.

A NEW BEGINNING

After the sale of The RoseBud, my life made a drastic change. For the first time in my life, I had no need to rise and shine early each morning. I had not belonged to clubs or organizations for all those years I had my store. I had been awarded honorary membership in Altrusa International of Temple, but I felt that they did not need me as an active member. They have a really well-oiled machine that never stops doing great things for our area. So as I was searching for a way to continue to serve my community, I decided that the Contemporaries of the Cultural Activities Center might have a spot for me.

Soon I heard rumors that Scott & White Hospital was making sounds about a new hospital for children. This was exciting. I have always loved little ones, and as a young child, I had been the survivor of double pneumonia. I often thought how lucky we were to have Dr. Happy Jack Swepston and his wonderful little hospital in my town, Rosebud, Texas.

PART V
ROSEBUD CHARACTERS

"Fashions fade, style is eternal."

—Yves Saint Laurent

OUR WORLD WAS A STAGE

Retail stores were our stage. Our parents, uncle and aunts were the main characters. We three kids were the players or extra characters. This was valuable training ground, and we all proved our characters over and over. We wore many hats and communicated with others in many ways. My dad was the one who was able to speak a variety of languages as he qualified as interpreter, and he kept all of us well-informed.

We learned to watch and listen. This proved to be very valuable. Working in the stores was certainly a family affair that allowed us, as a whole, to successfully communicate with folks from all ethnicities and walks of life.

Our lives were an important part of the whole production. And we all looked forward to each story. People were important to our family. All we desired was to treat everyone with love and respect and to say the words "thank you" over and over.

JESSIE GRACE TARVER

My special friend, Jessie Grace Tarver, was a petite little woman with salt-and-pepper hair and impressive dark eyebrows that framed her beautiful face. She had two grown sons when I knew her. I guess we got to know each other because Uncle Sol and Aunt Rose Cruvand lived across the street from the Tarvers. Since Mrs. Tarver had no daughters, I guess this was the reason she was attracted to me.

J.A. Tarver Sr. owned Planters National Bank, Tarver's Grocery Store, Tarver's Dry Goods, and was a partner with Sam Henslee in Tarver-Henslee Hardware. These stores were side by side and covered half the block. I don't remember Mr. Tarver as well as his wife and sons, and I believe he was a rather somber person—not a "city mover and shaker" like my Uncle Sol.

Mrs. Tarver's house was a big two-story mansion and quite a landmark in Rosebud, Texas. I heard that she lived her early years in Moody, Texas, a small community not far from Rosebud. She was a lady with good taste for decorating her elegant home. She was always well-dressed. She had a chauffeur who wore a dark-grey uniform and took her anywhere she wanted to go in her handsome navy-blue Packard automobile.

On Tuesday afternoons, the elegant auto pulled up to my house. The chauffeur came to the door to escort me to the car.

Rosebud Roses

We drove to Temple's Kyle Hotel and had a chocolate ice cream soda. We had so much to talk about each week. We returned to the Tarver house in Rosebud and played Sleeping Beauty.

She encouraged me to explore the desk drawer in her upstairs sunroom. The boys, Jack and John, always had a surprise for me. And then Mrs. Tarver would open her magic trunk filled with beautiful dolls from around the world, dressed in their native costumes. She told me that I was the only little girl who played with her dolls. I loved the stories she shared with me about faraway countries.

Mrs. Tarver wore beautiful clothes. On many occasions, she would have her chauffeur pull up to my dad's store. She never did get out of the car but had me bring exquisite white linen Palm Beach suits and Panama straw hats out to her. The suits were perfect for her petite figure. The skirts were long and slender. The jackets, with real pearl buttons, were fitted to the hip. Some had long, fitted sleeves, and some had short sleeves just above the elbow. The big Panama hats were gorgeous with her dark hair. She looked like a model who had just stepped off the pages of an exclusive magazine.

It was very hard on me when my beautiful Jessie Grace Tarver passed away. I had lost my most special friend. She was laid to rest in her lovely parlor in the stately Tarver home. Her sons placed a chair next to her casket and allowed me to watch over her. They knew how special our friendship was. Our favorite flower was the rose. Jack and John Albert were okay with me placing roses with her. I must have sat there for hours. I had lost my dear friend.

I remember getting dressed for our trips to Temple. I had the most gorgeous clothes because Aunt Pink created them from the finest fabrics in my parents' store. One very cold day, I chose to wear my beautiful pink lace Shirley Temple dress. When Mother said the weather was too cold for me to wear this fabulous dress,

I begged her to give in, saying I would wear my white wool coat over the dress. I won this confrontation but did not say a word about feeling a little chilled during our outing. But I always chose the clothes I wanted to wear. Looking back over the years, I realize how fortunate I was to have Aunt Pink. She was, without a doubt, a fabulous designer whose talent was very fine-tuned. She was way before her time. Ladies would love to have clothes like I was blessed to have as a child.

I realize how very lucky I was to be born into such a loving and brilliantly talented family. No wonder I ended up with the prestigious store, The RoseBud! It was truly my calling. I loved the opportunities I had to show ladies how beautiful they were or could be!

EL TAMPICO

Minnie and Carl Butler were an attractive couple, perfectly groomed from head to toe. They were the owners of El Tampico in Rosebud, Texas. Folks came from far and near to dine at this restaurant, enjoying the most delicious Mexican cuisine in the industry!

This popular eatery was housed in a pink stucco building on Rosebud's Main Street, with an impressive arched doorway leading into the spacious dining room with several elegant crystal chandeliers. There was also a generous dance floor.

I celebrated many birthdays at El Tampico! I could invite as many friends as I wanted, and Dad would put paper cups filled with nickels on the tables. We could play the jukebox for as long as we wished. These were such special times for my friends and me. We loved El Tampico, and I have yet to taste such delicious Mexican food anywhere else.

CLARENCE BOYD

Clarence Boyd was our mechanical professional who took special care of all the big automobiles in town. He was so impressive in his starched dress shirt, slacks and tie, topped off with his long white lab coat!

If our mother heard the slightest little noise in our big black Buick, she was sure to pay Clarence an emergency visit.

Clarence was a polished gentleman, and his closest friends were Lillian and Charlie Monroe (owners of Rosebud Drug) and Gussie Nell Davis (originator of the world-famous Kilgore Rangerettes).

Clarence Boyd was a very popular character in a quiet, reserved way.

DORA CRUZ

Dora Cruz was the most naturally beautiful Hispanic lady I have ever seen (and they are all beautiful). She was a dead ringer for Lana Turner, the movie star, except she had a rich olive complexion and dark-brown hair. Her eyes amazed me! I just loved to look at her. She was my hairstylist for many years!

An appointment with Dora was an exciting experience. I loved what she did with my hair! And, incidentally, she told me I was pregnant with my first son, two weeks before it was official! I think she was psychic! I just adored Dora!

Many years later, she came to the Temple RoseBud to visit and shop! We had a grand reunion! I still think about her often! Beautiful Dora!

CARRIE WEATHERBY

Carrie Weatherby lived in the yellow house next door to us. She was a small, willowy woman. She wore her light reddish-brown hair tightly permed. And she had dark-rimmed glasses! She was always happy. I looked forward to visiting with her.

When Carrie's husband died, she started a business of her own, sewing for the public. She created delicate organza blouses in pale shades of pink, blue, yellow, mint green, lavender and white. The design featured lace insertions and edging. When they were on display, they looked like the rainbow! I was her best advertisement—I had one of each! When I think of Carrie, I have to smile.

I had never known a preacher's wife who smoked! Not even a Methodist one!

THE DENTIST

I can picture Dr. L.A. Trubee in his dental office with the long sleeves to his dingy white dress shirt rolled tight above the elbows. He was a colorful character, and we all loved him. In addition to his work as the town dentist, he also delivered the *Dallas Morning News*.

I am almost sure that our mother had us to the dentist before we could walk. She was a firm believer in the old saying that "an ounce of prevention is worth a pound of cure." I remember her saying to Dr. Trubee, "You've got to sterilize your instruments before you work on my kids."

The dentist's son, Dean, lost a front tooth, so his Dad made him several teeth to replace this one. I still have a question about the Friday night football games when all the Rosebud players were on their knees searching for Dean's front tooth. Did he really lose his tooth, or were they using this as an excuse to rest?

Those were the days!

THE MONROES

The Rosebud Drug Store was owned by our odd couple. You would never put these two wonderful people together! Lillian was well-educated and very in-tune with our world. She was friendly and attractive. Mr. Charlie, or Dr. Charlie, as everyone called him, was a moody, grouchy old man, but he was a very highly respected pharmacist. We all depended on him to keep us well. I never saw a happy or positive look on his sour face, but we loved him anyway. The Drug Store was a popular place, and we all supported this business.

Evening in Paris was a popular fragrance. The packaging was absolutely beautiful, and the fragrance was addictive. The bottles were a rich, dark blue, and each container held a silk cord with fringe to match. Evening in Paris came in silver-boxed package sets. If one received this product as a gift—it was the ultimate! In Rosebud, Texas, it was available only at the Rosebud Drug!

Lillian Monroe's sister was the famous Gussie Nell Davis, originator of the internationally known Kilgore Rangerettes. Lillian was Gussie's only family, except for their niece, Betty. So when Gussie had time off from her very demanding job, she would visit the Monroes in Rosebud.

Gussie Nell Davis and I had a gift-wrapping business in the drug store during the Christmas holidays. I cannot begin to tell you how many Evening in Paris gift sets we wrapped for lucky young ladies! Our gift wraps were very elaborate, and it was nothing to sell a five-dollar gift wrap! This was expensive in those days.

On one occasion, Gussie and I decorated one of the drug store's windows with fifty Rangerette dolls! Our town loved it! We were all very loyal fans of Gussie's Kilgore Rangerettes! Many of us attended the New Year's Day Cotton Bowl Game in Dallas, Texas, just to see this amazing drill team perform at halftime!

The Monroes, Lillian and Charlie, were a special part of Rosebud, Texas!

Lillian and Charlie built a beautiful home in Rosebud with a six-foot brick-and-wood fence surrounding the property. When they celebrated their fiftieth anniversary, I got to help Gussie with the decorating. This was a fabulous party! It was the first time I ever saw a champagne fountain. And I will never forget this special event!

Lillian told me (when I was in middle school) that she would not be surprised if I grew up to be the editor of *Vogue* magazine! She had a way of making folks feel good.

MARSHALL H. CRUSE

He came sliding into the Sinclair service station on his motorcycle, crashed into the hedges and caught fire. Bob Thrasher was working there that day and witnessed the event. Bob quickly rushed over and pulled Marshall to safety.

Marshall was born to Florence McCullough and Marshall H. Cruse in Rosebud, Texas, on August 4, 1920. He and his brother Bill were very handsome men. Now that I think of it, there were many gorgeous guys and beautiful girls that grew up in our town.

Marshall was a captain in the US Air Force when he met the charming Heloise. He was stationed in China at this time. Marshall and Heloise married in 1948 while living in Nanking. From China, they moved to Waco, Texas.

I remember attending a luncheon in Waco featuring the famous Heloise as speaker. She was known for dyeing her hair in unusual colors. On this particular day, her hair was bright green. She was very entertaining, and I considered this one of my special days.

During their years of marriage, Heloise and Marshall had two children, Louis and Ponce. During his air force career, Lt. Col. Marshall Cruse was a jet fighter pilot living in Hawaii. My brother, Tom Tapman, who was also a fighter pilot, was stationed in Okinawa. Marshall paid Tom a special visit! (With Rosebud folks, age is certainly no barrier.)

Rosebud Roses

Heloise passed away in December of 1977. Her tombstone reads: "Heloise, Every Housewife's Friend." Her daughter, Ponce, continued her column, Hints from Heloise. She was the guest speaker for a Day for Women in Temple, Texas, in 2014. (This all-day event is made possible by the *Temple Daily Telegram*.) I had the opportunity to visit with Heloise (Ponce) and tell her that I personally knew her father, mother, Uncle Bill and grandmother, Florence.

I shared the story about Marshall at the Sinclair station and Bob pulling him to safety. She told me that she, too, rides a Harley motorcycle with a sidecar. When her dad, Marshall, found out, he said, "Oh, s---!" We had a great visit, exchanged phone numbers and agreed to meet in Rosebud someday for a walk down memory lane.

GUSSIE NELL DAVIS

Gussie Nell Davis was the originator of the internationally famous Kilgore College Rangerettes. She was born in Farmersville, Texas, on November 4, 1906. She attended college in Denton, at what is now known as Texas Woman's University, receiving a degree in physical education. She received a second college degree in education from the University of Southern California. Gussie's family dreamed of their daughter becoming a concert pianist. Gussie wanted to be a dancer.

She accepted a teaching position at Greenville High School. She was placed in charge of the pep squad. She developed the group into a team that performed on the football field at halftime in drum and bugle routines, which evolved into the "Flaming Flashes" drill team.

In 1939, Gussie Nell Davis came to Kilgore College, at the request of the board of regents, to develop a halftime show that would keep fans in their seats at halftime. This was a very conservative Bible Belt community, and some folks would go to their cars to sit out the halftime and enjoy a little "nip of whiskey." By 1940, the Kilgore Rangerettes were keeping fans in their seats with their precision moves and trademark high kicks! The Kilgore Rangerettes were gaining national attention!

Gussie retired in 1979 but continued to be active in her

community and garner many prestigious awards. In 1990, she was inducted into the Texas Women's Hall of Fame in Austin. The RoseBud in Temple had the honor of dressing her for this special occasion. Other prominent inductees included former First Lady Barbara Bush.

Joyce E. Pennington was instrumental in getting the world-famous Kilgore Rangerettes to perform in Temple, Texas, on two separate occasions at The RoseBud's annual Scott & White fashion show and luncheon at the Frank W. Mayborn Convention Center. Joyce footed the bill and also invited, as our very distinguished guest, Dr. Irving Dreibrodt, director emeritus of the Southern Methodist University Mustang Band!

Gussie Nell Davis died in her sleep in Kilgore, Texas, on December 20, 1993. She remains in the hearts of all the many young women and friends whose lives she touched...including her friend, that little girl in Rosebud.

Gina Balch from Gatesville was one of Gussie's outstanding Kilgore Rangerettes. I was blessed to work with this beautiful young lady as a contestant in the Miss Texas Pageant in Fort Worth. During the preparation for this competition, I had the honor of spending a couple of nights in the Rangerette dorm! What fun this was!

Gussie's sister, Lillian Monroe and husband Charlie, owned Rosebud Drug. Since they were Gussie's only family, Rosebud rightly claimed this famous lady who founded and organized the internationally famous Kilgore Rangerettes.

LEROY FICK

As Leroy was about to graduate from RHS, Mary Lee Stubbs, senior English Literature teacher, asked him if he had any plans. She said, "LeRoy, if I could get you a scholarship, would you go to college?" She got the scholarship, and LeRoy was off to Lon Morris College, where he graduated with honors. He enrolled in school at the University of Texas and earned a degree in engineering. He went to work for Brown and Root and was the lead engineer on the Livingston Dam and the twenty-four-mile toll bridge of the Lake Pontchartrain Causeway from Metarie to Ponchatoula. LeRoy also designed a heliport in Egypt.

There were no limitations on this man's talent. He was proud of his heritage. He called Gene Linn and asked if he would lead the tour of Rosebud's Main Street. He was bringing his family to town for a little Rosebud history. Gene Linn is a walking encyclopedia for our town. The Fick family came away very impressed with the little town their husband and dad grew up in—thank you, Gene Linn!

TOM FORD

Our famous nephew, Tom Ford, the fashion designer, grew up as Thomas Carlyle Ford, the son of Shirley Thrasher, Bob's baby sister, and Tom Ford Sr. Tom is especially remembered for his phenomenal revival of the Gucci label. Tom is famous in his own right, for his internationally known Tom Ford label. He also directed the Oscar-nominated film *A Single Man.*

Tom was a very bright young boy. It was obvious that he was destined for great accomplishments. He is also a very handsome man. Tom was a frequent visitor to Rosebud during his young years. Nettie Grace Bailey and Frank Berkett Thrasher were his grandparents. Of course, the whole family claimed kin to this bright new star in the world of fashion and films.

Tom grew up in Austin, Texas, and Santa Fe, New Mexico. Today he has homes all over the country. His mother and sister, Jennifer, and family reside in California.

ROBERT ROYAL LUCAS

The Lucas family had a little short-order restaurant on Main Street, very close to my dad's store. Everyone loved Royal Lucas. (We called him Bob.) After graduation from RHS, this handsome young man made his way to Waco and Baylor University. He worked his way through college washing dishes at Luby's Cafeteria and doing other small jobs. Upon graduation from BU, he went to work at IBM in Dallas. IBM sent him to Houston and back to Dallas. Bob did very well at IBM.

Bob met a very special lady, Betty Hall, while at Baylor. He married this pretty girl from Mount Pleasant in East Texas. Betty was a good sport. She was smart and very attractive. Even though she would fish and hunt with the guys, she was, at the same time, a very polished woman. They had two wonderful sons, Bruce and Steven, and both of them worked for IBM.

The war had everyone's attention. Bob joined the US Air Force and became a bomber pilot. He and his crew flew thirteen missions before their plane was damaged and they were able to get on the ground. They hid by day and walked at night in order to stay safe. They had some close calls before finally reaching Switzerland. The important thing is that they made it home. Bob remembers when they saw the Statue of Liberty, they were about to burst with pride.

Rosebud Roses

As they came off their plane, they kissed the ground and were so glad to be Americans!

Bob climbed the IBM ladder to success. He was a war hero! Bob Lucas was a financial success, but most importantly, he and Betty were our special friends. My Bob and I would meet them in Waco for homecoming celebrations at Baylor. We always had to treat ourselves to a beer in a frosted mug at the famous Harry B's!

Through the many years of our close friendship, the two Bobs and their sons—Bruce and Steve, and Bobby and Mike—hunted and fished together. We two Bettys had other fun things to do like lunch and shopping.

THE MCATEES

David R. McAtee, son of Chevrolet dealer LeeRay and Florene McAtee, grew up in Rosebud, Texas. He and his wife, Kay, restored the Chevrolet building on Main Street and freshened up D Brown Library with repairs and new paint. Kay brought the Wells house, purchased many years ago by the McAtees, back to its original glory. Jane and I were invited to tour the house during a Golden Years Reunion. We were thrilled to visit the home of Jane's grandmother and to see its tremendous and tasteful renovation. Kay is a talented lady.

Their son, David R. McAtee II, had already had a colorful career in the practice of law when *Texas Monthly* honored this father and son as one of the most outstanding father-son teams in the state of Texas.

David R. McAtee II was appointed as senior executive vice president and general counsel of AT&T, effective as of October 1, 2015. Mr. McAtee was formerly a partner of Haynes and Boone, LLP.

David Sr. was awarded the Outstanding Alumnus Award by the Rosebud High School Golden Years Reunion committee. This is truly a big honor.

Rosebud is very proud of the beautiful and talented McAtee family.

BERT NUSSBAUM

Bert Nussbaum was very smart and paid strict attention to detail. After working thirty-three years with Continental Grain Company, he and his wife, Joy, came back to the Rosebud area. For a while, Bert worked for A.T. Garrett, driving a tractor. He became the justice of the peace for Rosebud, but this only lasted two weeks. He just could not pronounce folks dead.

This is the man who was in charge of loading two ships and nine hundred boxcars with quality wheat to ship out of Newport News, Virginia.

Bert led our RHS Golden Years Reunion group as our president. He was one in a million. We could never have paid for this man's true worth.

Bert and Joy retired for the last time and moved to Garden Estates Retirement Center in Temple, Texas. They were killed in an auto accident in front of Star Hall on their way to Rosebud.

ROBERT LEE MCCLENDON

Robert Lee McClendon was born in 1919. After graduating from RHS, he attended Tyler Community College and learned Morse code. He joined the merchant marines in 1942 and served as a radio operator. He was sent to Puerto Rico and back to New Orleans. In WWII, Robert was a radio operator in the US Coast Guard. Learning Morse code had paid off.

As a boy, Robert worked hard, long hours on his family's dairy farm. He excelled as an Eagle Scout. (Byron Stubbs was his scoutmaster.) His work experiences were many. He worked at the Ford Motor Company assembly plant in Dallas. Robert worked in the shipyard in Houston. Back in Dallas, he serviced a bubble gum and peanut route with two hundred and fifty stops in Dallas. And then he started Mac's Service and Supplies, where he founded Scotch Plaid Inc., a major detergent manufacturing company for the car wash industry. He became a financial success. He sold his company in 1985. Robert was a Christian man and a member of the Church of Christ in Dallas.

Robert's wife died in 2003. Her name was Dorothy Jonan, another Rosebud native. Robert and his second wife, Grace, had three children and one grandchild. Robert passed away on

Rosebud Roses

December 20, 2012. We will forever be proud of this Rosebud success story, Robert Lee McClendon.

(Another Rosebud product, Gene Linn, shared information about Robert with me.)

RED MURFF

The Scout: Searching for the Best in Baseball chronicles Red Murff's remarkable thirty-three-year career (1933–1960) as perhaps the most successful talent scout in history, signing over two hundred players to professional contracts, according to coauthor Mike Capps.

Working for the Houston Colt .45s, New York Mets, Montreal Expos, Chicago Cubs and Atlanta Braves, Murff drove over a million miles to pluck young, unknown ballplayers from obscurity. His recruits include four of the great 1969 world champion New York Mets: Nolan Ryan, Jerry Koosman, Jerry Grote and Kenny Boswell.

Red Murff graduated from Rosebud High School with my husband, Bob Thrasher. One year, while attending our RHS Golden Years Reunion, Red said, "Bob Thrasher, you beat me out of my place on our football team."

Bob replied, "It didn't hurt you too bad." Bob's favorite sport was baseball.

Red Murff is a legend, and Rosebud is part of him.

Red passed away at his home in Tyler, Texas. (His younger brother, Edward, was my classmate.)

Red's book, *The Scout*, is a thrilling story about America's favorite sport, written by the real pro, Red Murff!

The field at Mary Hardin-Baylor is named for this great sportsman.

HENRY SKUPIN

Henry wrote a wonderful book about his life on the farm near Rosebud, Texas. The title was *Growing Up on the Farm*. He was born in 1942 to sharecropping parents. Soon after, they moved to the self-supporting farm where he actually grew up. He graduated from Texas A&M and worked for Texaco developing seismic software in Houston, Texas; New Orleans, Louisiana; and Tulsa, Oklahoma. He lives with his wife in Houston.

His book has enabled its readers to revisit exciting experiences from those times with later generations. Sharing Henry's book with old-timers has opened wonderful conversations with family and friends and a world of wonderful stories never told before. What a delight!

I asked Henry for advice about publishing a book. He was very generous, and I love referring to the vital information he was so willing to share with me!

I encourage everyone to read Henry's book!

BILL ED STALLWORTH

Little Billy Ed Stallworth was a graduate of Rosebud High School. He entered Tarleton State College, and in 1954 he graduated from Texas A&M College with a BA in architectural construction. After serving two years in the United States Air Force in Korea, he joined Brown and Root, where he worked in Venezuela, Brazil, the Middle East and London, England.

Lt. Bill Stallworth married Jackie Gwen Wardlaw in 1957. They had two children, William and Suzanne. In 1980, the family made Houston their home.

Little Billy Ed Stallworth was president of Brown and Root Inc. in Houston. In 1986, Bill founded an engineering and construction consulting firm that provides services in the international oil and construction industries.

Bill served on the board of directors of Fugro N.V., a multinational consulting company. He also served on the board of advisors for Texas A&M's Center for International Business Studies.

It is especially sad that he was awarded the Outstanding Alumnus Award from the Rosebud High School Golden Years Reunion in April 2016, after he was deceased. How I wish he could have known how proud we are of Billy Ed Stallworth, the son of Maudine, the school teacher, and Ira, the mail carrier.

His wife, Jackie, and sister, Jeanette, preceded him in death. Bill passed away December 4, 2014. He and Tom Tapman were good friends.

ROBERT SUMMERS

Robert Summers was a very popular item on the scene in Rosebud, Texas. All the girls were attracted to him, but Robert was not so quick to react to this attention. He grew up in a great family. Everyone adored his mother, Ruth, a tiny little lady, full of energy. Robert had two brothers, Flemming and Jack. He had one sister, Annie Ruth.

Robert went on to the University of Texas after graduation from RHS. He was a basketball star at Texas and played in Madison Square Garden, New York. This was quite a thrill for all the folks in Rosebud, Texas.

Robert was such a good, genuine person. He was admired by so many folks. He now lives in San Antonio with his precious daughter.

We talk on the phone occasionally. It is important to stay in touch. We have fun remembering the good old days in Rosebud.

VERA WARROCK

At one time, the Warrocks owned the *Rosebud News*, before selling it to the J.R. Kilgore family. Vera Warrock was a natural in the news business, and she brought a very special flavor to the town. She was a vivacious lady who never married. She was known as a great entertainer, in serious demand for professional appearances.

Vera was well known all over the country for her magnificent miniature elephant collection. Each one had its own personal story. Many were prized gifts from world travelers and our servicemen who were stationed in all parts of the world. These little figures were extremely interesting, and some were dressed in precious jewels! Folks came from everywhere to view this marvelous collection, and Vera was so glad to share her good fortune.

The story goes around that Vera did a mini striptease atop her grand piano at a glamorous party hosted in her stately two-story home in Rosebud! Now this is just hearsay, and most folks would not be surprised if she started the rumor herself!

I don't know how I was lucky enough to be one of the "keepers of the collection," but I do not remember having any limits on my frequent visits to see Miss Vera and the elephants. (As a seasoned adult, I have a larger-than-life fascination with elephants today!)

Many years later, when Bob and I had announced our wedding plans, Miss Vera asked to personally attend to our wedding write-up. This was quite an honor!

Miss Vera Warrock was indeed a colorful character!

DANIEL DAVID ZABCIK

Daniel David Zabcik was valedictorian of his 1946 Rosebud High School class. He graduated from the University of Texas at Austin with a Bachelor of Science degree in civil engineering.

Daniel first served in the United States Army and then as an officer in the US Air Force. He served two and a half years in Okinawa, earning a Korean Service Medal. He was discharged in 1953.

Daniel worked for Lockwood and Andrews, a Houston-based engineering firm. He later joined Metallic Building Company in Houston. This was a metal building manufacturing company, where he began his long and ultimately highly accomplished career. His wife, Joyce Wells of Port Arthur, passed away in 1986. They had three children, Carol, Dan and Bob.

Later Dan became reacquainted with his Rosebud High School sweetheart, Rosemary Ligon Hancock. Dan became stepfather to Millard, Mary, Larry and Arthur Hancock.

After Dan retired from NCI Building Systems in 1991, he served on the board of directors of this same company until 1998. His career with NCI spanned more than three decades, helping to lead this company from humble beginnings to its place as an industry giant.

Dan grew up on a farm near Rosebud. He was an outdoors

man who enjoyed fishing, golfing, hiking and birding. He loved mountain, desert and coastal settings. The call of the wild always found him ready to join family and friends to enjoy his favorite sports.

Dan passed away on August 17, 2016, in Houston, Texas.

ERNESTINE GREEN

I remember Ernestine as a tall, slender, very attractive young lady with a beautiful complexion and short medium-blond hair. She was an intellectual student all through school.

Ernestine was an impeccable dresser who favored well-designed tailored fashion. She was a serious-minded intellect. There was no doubt that she was destined for great accomplishments.

And, sure enough, she ended up in Washington, D.C., as a personal secretary to Congressman Bob Poage.

Ernestine was a bright star who hailed from Rosebud, Texas—a small town with big achievers.

FAMOUS ATHLETES

Rosebud claimed several well-known athletes through the years.

A.D. Whitfield Jr. played football with the Washington Redskins.

Brian Parcus played baseball for Texas A&M.

John Sebeck, SMU basketball captain, was killed in a Navy trainer plane. John was a man with a host of friends. He was special to us in Rosebud, Texas.

LaDainian Tomlinson was a superstar for the San Diego Chargers. This Rosebud native was one of the greatest running backs in the history of the National Football League. He is a good person who is very proud of his Falls County roots. And we are very proud of him.

The Rosebud Roses were a semi-pro baseball team with coach-manager Red Muldrow and Bully Parcus as pitcher. Johnny Storey was a member of this team. When we put all the details together, it becomes a real love story with red roses!

SADNESS

Yes, we had some sadness too. A young sailor was murdered on his way home to visit family. The whole town was grief-stricken that such a horror could touch our town. He was such a sweet kid from a wonderful family. I will never forget his precious smile. His dad kept yards manicured to perfection, and his mom was a talented seamstress.

Kenneth Allen McDuff was a disgrace to Rosebud, Texas. He was a vicious murderer that had absolutely no respect for humanity. We should have known he was headed to commit the most horrendous crimes by his behavior in school. He left a huge black mark on our town that it did not deserve.

Kenneth Allen McDuff was a misfit. We will forever grieve for his defenseless victims. They never had a chance to survive.

PART VI
SCOTT & WHITE

"Don't be into trends. Don't make fashion own you, but you decide what you are, what you want to express by the way you dress and the way you live."

—Gianni Versace

HOSPITAL TOURS

Remember when nurses wore crisp white uniforms, starched so they rustled when they walked? Their white silk hosiery and lace-up shoes were an important part of the uniform. The black stripe on her cap told us that she was an RN. When the weather was cold, she would wrap herself in that beautiful navy-blue cape lined in red. This was a sight to behold! She was our angel of mercy.

There were times when I felt I should have earned my own black stripe to celebrate all the hospital tours I pulled. Since I was the oldest child in our family, taking care of the sick folks in our family was an honor, and I was always close by.

The first experience was when Aunt Rose came to Rosebud High School to see me in a school production. She fell down two flights of cement stairs. Both legs were broken above and below the knees. I was crushed as I rode in the ambulance with her to King's Daughters Hospital in Temple. Our friend, Dr. Chernoskey, met us at the emergency room. The breaks were so bad that pins had to be inserted in both legs. Her attitude was positive, but life would never be the same. Walking was difficult, and her legs were always wrapped in elastic bandages. Pretty shoes were a thing of the past.

There were a few times when both Mother and Aunt Rose were

Betty Thrasher

in two different hospitals—Aunt Rose in Marlin and Mother in Rosebud. I kept the road hot between the two towns.

Aunt Pink and Uncle Boss were unable to live safely in their Cameron home. Mother and I helped to relocate them to the New Heritage House in Rosebud. When they became ill and had to be in the hospital, I shared time there with Mother and Aunt Johnnye. The Fords were precious people, and they had lovingly cared for older family members. We all wanted to take good care of this sweet couple.

Aunt Dora was at Heritage House when she had to be taken to Scott & White Hospital in Temple. It was much easier for me and my brother to care for her in Gatesville. My friend, Inez Arnold, made a room available for her in the rest home, where she later passed away. She was happy here because she was surrounded by family.

Mother's situation was different. She had surgery at Hillcrest in Waco, recuperated at our home in Gatesville for about six months and decided it was time to go home to Rosebud. After three weeks there, she suffered a heart attack and was in the Halbert Hospital in Rosebud. Very unexpectedly, she passed away here.

HILLCREST HOSPITAL

The RoseBud had an urgent phone call from a lady at Hillcrest Hospital in Waco. The store that had committed to fit models for their fashion show had closed its doors and gone out of business. The show was scheduled to take place at Ridgewood Country Club in two weeks. Of course, The RoseBud would be happy and very honored to step in and help. We immediately went to work scheduling fittings for the models. Needless to say, the models were delightful, and the show was a huge success. Everything was perfect, and we answered the call to do this show for Hillcrest the next two years.

Today, Hillcrest is a member of Baylor Scott & White Hospital Group. We have a wonderful relationship. My daughter-in-law, Patti, and I were escorted on a tour of the beautiful Hillcrest Hospital and were most impressed. It is a fabulous facility that we can all be proud of. It is a credit to Waco, Texas.

THE CASTLE ON THE HILL

When we brought The RoseBud to Temple, Texas, in 1981, I had never had any dealings with Scott & White Hospital. My allegiance was with Coryell Memorial Hospital in Gatesville and the two Lowreys—E.E. and O.W. These brothers were as near genius as any human being can be classified. E.E., or Ellsworth, was always smiling, while O.W., or Wendell, was extremely serious and rare to recognize anyone in his presence. However, Wendell was one of the very best diagnosticians in the vast medical world. Ellsworth was sweet-natured and friendly. But in summation, both were fantastic doctors, highly respected by patients, peers and friends. Gatesville was blessed to have such special men of medicine. (Their father was also a physician, and their mother, Kate, was a friend to many.)

My first visit to Scott & White Hospital came on the day of my brother's official retirement from the United States Air Force! I was bursting with pride as I attended his retirement ceremony at Fort Hood. Afterwards, I felt very sick, and as we left this event, my husband drove me straight to Scott & White.

Suddenly, rashes began to appear all over my body—three different kinds of rashes. The first doctor to see me was Dr. Douglas Hurley. Shortly after, a young doctor named Robert A. Probe came by. He sat down and talked with me for quite a while.

I was quite impressed with this young doctor and have followed him in his highly successful career. He left us for more intense study but returned to S&W to become chairman of orthopedics (later chairman of the board of directors) and is currently chief medical officer of the Baylor Scott and White System.

I was fifty-three years of age when I went on my first ski adventure. Our son, Dr. Michael Thrasher, and his wife, Patti, invited Bob and me to spend a week in Breckenridge, Colorado, along with Patti's parents, Rozelle and J.C. Van Dyke. We also had our two grandsons, little Aaron and Jeffery. Bob, J.C. and I enrolled in ski school. (Rozelle was babysitting little Aaron.) I had no business being there! I snow-plowed to a stop and heard a very loud "pop!"

I had critically injured my left knee. The doctor in Denver could perform the necessary surgery, but I would not be able to go home until the end of the week. The RoseBud was a new business in Temple, so I elected to return to S&W. We arrived at the ER very late at night and returned to the clinic to see a doctor the next day.

I could go on forever about our Scott & White Hospital. I love this amazing Mayo of the Southwest. We have all been blessed to know many of the fine doctors personally.

We've seen many changes through the years. Bob had serious vascular surgery, and I will never forget that after long hours in the OR, our Dr. Clifford Buckley was standing by Bob's bed at ten o'clock that night. I call that dedication.

We asked Dr. Jim Chandler, whom we loved and admired as a personal friend as well as our doctor, to put us in touch with the best "first-string" surgeon for my dad's colon operation. When we reported to John Hendrick's office, we actually got the best, and there was exciting evidence of his fabulous football career. We dearly love this guy.

Betty Thrasher

The day after the 9/11 tragedy that took down the twin towers in New York City, Bob had a stroke. (I had witnessed two customers in The RoseBud having the start of a stroke.) I knew the signals and rushed Bob to the Scott & White ER. Because we arrived at the hospital so soon, Bob came through twelve days in the hospital with no ill effects. Thank God for this blessing.

RELOCATED

A young man came to my room with a wheelchair to transport me to therapy. It was a grueling workout, and I was exhausted. When the man returned me to my room, it was completely empty, stripped of all furniture and personal belongings. I looked at the young man and asked, "Where is everything? Did I die?" He was totally speechless, and neither of us knew what to do or where to go! My heart skipped a beat.

I had been very ill, and my stay in the hospital had been extended. A nurse came running toward us and said I was being moved to another room. The hospital had been redecorating a couple of rooms, and they were just like new! The staff had relocated all my belongings and furniture to a bright, new, clean room. Surprise! What a sweet thing to do.

The wheelchair driver and I were elated!

THE DOCTORS

Dr. Alfred B. Knight brought such tremendous growth to Scott & White as president from 2000–2011. His wife, Nan, was such a great asset.

John and Mark Montgomery are a father-son team of great doctors.

Jim Chandler was a genius and one of Scott & White's best doctors.

Jack Eberts always wore a smile and said that after retirement, he would like to be the doorman at The RoseBud.

Bob Myers was president of S&W Hospital for more than ten years. He was the most popular pediatrician in Temple, loved by everyone.

Jack Myers followed in Dad's footsteps and is popular with patients of all ages and one smart, dedicated doctor and family man.

John Hendricks is our first-string all-American surgeon.

Bob Carabasi is one of the kindest people. He took good care of my dad. He is a very special gentleman and a very good doctor.

Phillip Cain retired from S&W, and his patients were all mad at him. He is a great doctor and a good man. We will miss him.

Bill Hamilton was an all-American in UT football, and that's the way we see him at S&W.

Rosebud Roses

Kirby Hitt is the man in the knee replacement business. He is a great doctor who is always in demand, in spite of being an Aggie!

Bill and Kirby are a fantastic team!

Bob Probe just keeps climbing to the top at S&W. He and Barbara are highly respected physicians.

Wade Knight can steal your heart, or better, he can make it tick, but he says he is retiring.

Paxton Howard is loving retirement, and in his spare time, he makes a great Uncle Sam!

André Avots is keeping S&W's board intact. He's the doc with the great personality that we all admire.

Patsy Sulac is doing a great job keeping young folks informed and the more mature ones practicing good habits. She is such a dynamic personality and has made a very important impact on all of us!

Two of Betty's favorite guys, Dr. Bill Hamilton and Dr. Kirby Hitt, at the Southwest Conference fashion show.

DOWN THE HILL

Bob decided to take me outside for a ride in the old-fashioned tall-back wheelchair. I was wearing my hospital gown and covering my legs with just a sheet. We bravely ventured outside on this clear, cool day. As we strolled down the sidewalk, the big, old, heavy chair took control and began pulling us down the slanting walk. We were moving too fast, unable to stop! When we reached the end of the walk, the chair slammed into a cement curb and nearly pitched me over and out. I don't even remember how Bob got me and this dinosaur chair back inside the hospital.

This chair needed to be retired.

CALL MY MOTHER

The Montgomery family amazes me! Dr. John and Alma have left their mark on the good life in Temple, Texas! Alma and I became friends when she came to the store to shop. I will never forget an incident when I was not feeling well. She and John were on a trip out of town. When they reached their destination, Alma and John called to check on me.

The Montgomerys' son, Mark, is also a doctor. One day I called to see if I could speak to him. The secretary said he was unavailable, so would I like to leave a message? I answered, "No, I'll just call his mother." It wasn't any time until Mark called me.

I told this story and my primary physician, Dr. Jack Myers, said, "Betty, if you need me and are unable to reach me, just call my mom!" His mother, Katherine, is a RoseBud model and dear friend.

I adore these families. The whole group is very special and multitalented.

FASHION SHOWS

For more than twenty years, The RoseBud staged major benefit fashion shows for Scott & White Hospital and Children's Miracle Network.

These shows were presented at the Frank W. Mayborn Convention Center in Temple, Texas. As many as fifty models have given their time, beauty and talent to this cause. The models are selected by The RoseBud. They are not paid for their participation; it is given from the heart. They even bought tickets to the events.

As many as one hundred business and professional men in the community put on their classic tuxedos to serve the tables or sell raffle tickets. They are a very popular part of these events. The guests in attendance love these guys!

Jon Dungan contributed his time and talent to supply equipment and manpower to make our shows technically outstanding, and we all owe him a huge debt of gratitude. Thanks so much, Jon!

Our generous merchants supported these fundraisers with gifts and money. The *Temple Daily Telegram* and KCEN-TV willingly gave us the much-needed publicity. It was always exciting to open the newspaper the next day, see the photos and read the reviews, then hear the comments on TV.

The RoseBud only did fashion shows for fundraisers. We were

invited to present shows at various country clubs in Waco, Bryan, Lago Vista and Austin.

The first show in Austin was at Onion Creek Country Club for legislative wives. We were invited back numerous times. The Legends golf tournaments were held there. We had numerous shows at Barton Creek Country Club for various occasions. We probably did the most shows for the Austin Country Club. On one occasion, we brought a show to the Austin Club for the wives of legislators. Ballet Austin invited us on several occasions. We had many friends and customers in Austin, including Symphony Guild. We always loved going to Austin.

The show at Ridgewood Country Club in Waco became a regular event benefitting Waco Historic Foundation. The RoseBud filled in for Hillcrest Hospital one year. They were scheduled to present a show with a local store, who went out of business about two weeks before the show was to take place at Ridgewood. When we were contacted to step in and present the show, it was our pleasure to do so. We were invited to do this show the next two years for Hillcrest.

Baylor University asked us to supply the entertainment for a fashion show one year. This certainly pleased me. I had served on an advisory board at this university for many years, and it was a pleasure to work with them. I loved the fashion design and marketing students. Sometimes we presented their original designs in our shows. Dr. Judith Lusk became one of our regular models.

SCOTT & WHITE FASHION SHOWS

The Scott & White Auxiliary, recognized by the name Yellow Birds, was in charge of the food and decorations. The cost of the ticket for our first show was $6.75. I worked diligently, for many years, to explain that the price of the ticket was wholly a donation to the cause and not a fee for lunch or the fashion show. Our waiters were known as the "Men in Tux."

The RoseBud spared no cost for putting on the glamorous show. This was our baby, and we would certainly foot the bill for the show. Models and Men in Tux did not get paid, and if they planned to have lunch, they bought a ticket. Jon Dungan graciously ran the technical part of this event without a charge. Some of his crew came from Austin, donating their time and talent as a favor to Jon. These men gave us the very best in lighting and sound technology. They were very valuable to the success of the show.

The Fountain of Beauty, led by Karen Dungan, created the latest in hairstyles for our models. Angela Allen and Gaylene Galloway, along with the Lancôme artists from Temple Mall Dillard's, donated their time for the most beautiful makeup. The models were just gorgeous. We would only use our RoseBud customers on our runways.

The RoseBud began selecting the finest in fashion and

accessories months ahead of the show. We were in great demand to present shows around the country because, quite simply, we were the best in the business and the word circulated quickly. Our vendors at market were strong supporters and donated fabulous gifts to be given away during the shows. Many of these friends from Dallas and New York markets attended our shows. This was a huge compliment to us all. The RoseBud also gave three $500 gift certificates.

Glass the Florist in Cameron cultivated beautiful containers of vivid-colored mums to center each table, at a very minimum cost to the auxiliary. Annie Ruth and Donald Glass were personal friends of mine and Scott & White Hospital. This accommodation was above and beyond the call of duty.

As the attendance grew, it was obvious that the luncheon menu seriously needed great improvement. It was not easy to increase our ticket price to forty dollars, but it must be done. A show like ours should have had the price of one hundred dollars. Remember, this was a benefit!

The event kept on growing, and we had reached a capacity crowd. We had a waiting list for Men in Tux. Ladies from out of town were wanting to model. Scott & White was approaching its one hundredth birthday. The RoseBud was planning an even more extravagant show.

And then a letter arrived from the president of the Scott & White Auxiliary saying they had decided that their group would be too busy to have the annual Holiday Extravaganza. I could not believe my eyes! I was amazed that they had not paid me a visit as a courtesy for all those years of hard work. I didn't know this at the time, but I really had not needed to worry. We were flooded with requests to sponsor our show.

Children's Miracle Network was chosen as the sponsor for our show. Together, we were even more fabulous for the next five years. These folks were great to work with. I called on my friends at the CAC for help! The Contemporaries quickly came to my aid, and they were professionals at decorating. The Mayborn Convention Center was out-of-this-world gorgeous, thanks to Choni Pischinger and her very able crew. (The auxiliary had requested that we not refer to our waiters as Men in Tux, because this was their property.) The new title for our handsome waiters was a little more sophisticated. They would be referred to as Black Tie Guys. They showed up en masse and did a wonderful job!

Our last big show was a huge success. I had finally convinced Grace Jones to be our guest. It was both fitting and proper to honor her for bringing the world of haute couture to Central Texas. We invited Joan Brashear to escort Grace to the show and bring her to The RoseBud afterward, so folks could visit with her. I think she had a great time.

All through the years, the show was outstanding. Our models were the best—we preferred to use real people and never had professional models on The RoseBud runways. The show themes were quite varied.

Grace Jones and Betty at the Arthur Brashear home.

TRAVEL POSTERS

One of our fashion shows, Holiday Extravaganza, a benefit for Scott & White Memorial Hospital in Temple, Texas, featured travel. We dressed models in a variety of fashions from countries around the world, with models carrying travel posters to match the outfit. This was just one of our opening scenes for this annual fundraiser for our fabulous hospital. Geiger from Austria was a huge favorite of The RoseBud. We adored the representative, Liz White. Mr. Geiger himself came to the US one year to visit three of his best accounts. The RoseBud was one of the three! This was a great honor, and for years we received chocolates filled with liqueurs every Christmas! One year, we received a magnificent brass display rack from Mr. Geiger. The fabrics in the Geiger clothes were gorgeous, and the workmanship, design and customer appeal were great. We loved doing business with this fine company.

Patti, Barbara and I loved to visit the Geiger showrooms in Dallas and New York! And I got to visit the company in Austria while on an extended trip to Europe.

Each model carried a travel poster from her country. Our area boasts the fact that many of our folks are world travelers. We had to be ready to accommodate their needs. We always recommended a Burberry coat with zip-out lining. This would be a blessing in rain, sleet, snow or sun! Portolino leather gloves lined in silk or cashmere were a must! Kaminski's packable hats were a blessing because they could be rolled and packed away in one's luggage. We loved gorgeous, as well as practical, bags like Bally of Switzerland to carry all those necessary items like credit cards and lipstick! All a lady needed to complete this picture was a good, comfortable pair of closed-in shoes and a pair of wonderful boots! Of course, we recommended black for shoes, hats and handbags. Gloves could be any color, but we invariably chose black, fashion's practical and smart choice! All that we needed to complete this picture was luggage and a plane ticket!

THE KILGORE COLLEGE RANGERETTES

Joyce Pennington, American Drill Team owner, brought the internationally famous Kilgore College Rangerettes to Temple, Texas, on two separate occasions to perform at The RoseBud Fashion Show benefitting Scott & White Hospital. Joyce knew Gussie Nell Davis, the originator of this popular group. (Joyce purchased Gussie's business.) Joyce hosted this meticulous team of remarkable and talented ladies and their coaches in Salado overnight. What a gift! Many former Rangerettes attended our show in support of Scott & White, as well as their alma mater!

The Kilgore Rangerettes are world famous and highly regarded in the United States and abroad. Their founder, Gussie Nell Davis, was my personal friend, so it was especially exciting to share this fabulous talent on The RoseBud's runway in Temple, Texas.

The internationally famous Rangerettes at The RoseBud fashion show benefitting Scott & White.

TEXAS A&M YELL LEADERS

The Southwest Conference was the focal point of one Scott & White show. We searched the area to find an impressive list of outstanding former college athletes living in the Temple area. We had football, basketball, baseball, track, tennis and golf celebrities in our midst.

The Texas A&M Yell Leaders came, brought mascot Reveille and performed for us. We had all the Southwest Conference schools represented, and we featured all their fight songs as they paraded The RoseBud runway!

Dr. Bill Hamilton is an all-American football star from the University of Texas. Dr. Kirby Hitt played football at A&M. Dr. Paul Diekert was a great A&M golfer. Dr. Ralph Person was an all-American track star and big man on campus at the University of Texas, and he was pastor of the First Presbyterian Church in Temple. H.K. Allen wore his football jersey from his days on the team at UT. (His coach was my friend, Billy Gilstrap.)

MILLENNIUM MAGIC

Millennium Magic embraced the coming century on The RoseBud runway for a Children's Miracle Network fundraiser. The scene was the Frank W. Mayborn Convention Center in Temple, Texas, in October 1999.

A candy apple–red Harley roared up onto the runway driven by Dr. Jim Madsen! He was instantly surrounded by gorgeous models in glamorous red fashions. A total of $31,316 was raised this day for Scott & White Hospital. The RoseBud was celebrating its twentieth anniversary.

We turned the clock back to bring some elegant fashions from 1981–1988 in order to prove that classic fashion never, ever goes out of style! Whittall and Shon exotic hats were featured just for fun. Friends from the fashion industry—Renfrew, Berman and Associates; Brad Hughes and Associates; Lori Veith Sales; Double D Ranchwear; and Bill Strain's Temple Art Gallery donated fantastic door prizes.

An elaborate array of exotic fireworks brought the show to a climax with the crowd loving all the fanfare and commotion.

"THE MOST WONDERFUL TIME OF THE YEAR"

September 11, 2001, brought all of us to our knees in mourning after the horrendous terrorist attacks on the twin towers of the World Trade Center in New York City. Our Holiday Extravaganza plans had been finalized, and we knew that the show had to go on as planned.

As always, our handsome United States Marines posted the colors, and no one could hold back the tears as we watched these special young men in their beautiful blue military uniforms. I could hardly speak, and all I could say was, "We will never forget 9/11, but we must move on. We will come together, stronger than ever, stand united and know that we are blessed to live in the greatest country in the world—the United States of America."

Miss Texas, Stacey James, sang our national anthem and asked the crowd to join her in the Pledge of Allegiance to our beautiful flag. Special guests were our own local heroes and protectors—the firemen and policemen. Miss Texas honored their presence with "God Bless America."

This was our nineteenth year to present this annual October fundraiser, "The Most Wonderful Time of the Year." Our sponsors were McLane Company Inc., Texas State Optical, Cefco,

KCEN-TV, Bank of America and Scott & White Hospital. All proceeds from this event benefitted Children's Miracle Network.

Special guest was Grace Jones of Salado, recognized for her outstanding contribution to fashion in Central Texas. Lunch was catered by Word of Mouth in Austin. Eighty business and professional men donned their black tuxedos as our famous Black Tie Guys and served champagne to the guests.

As always, Lancôme of the Temple Mall Dillard's created models' makeup, while Fountain of Beauty styled models' hair. These folks are real professionals.

Karen and Rudy Gonzalez of Leander joined their students—the Penningtons, the Goforths, the Moores and the McConnells—on stage for a beautiful waltz.

YELLOW ROSE

October 2002 marked the end of the annual Scott & White Hospital fundraiser shows. This was a sad day for those of us who had been so involved for all those twenty years. To this day, I do not know what possessed me to wear that black cocktail hat.

Before the show was to begin, I was told that Secret Service agents were roaming all over the building, and of course, I was very suspicious of what was going on, until I was told that our First Lady of Texas, Anita Perry, was there! This really was impressive, and I felt so honored to have her attend our show! (Why, oh why, did I not get rid of that silly hat?) I had never ever worn a hat to my shows before, and actually, I forgot I had one on. I kind of thought the crowd would get a kick out of the hat, but—the joke was on me! (I must have been photographed more on this day than ever before!)

Mrs. Perry presented me with the Yellow Rose of Texas Award for community service. As if this wasn't enough, Donny Sequin presented me with the Spirit to Serve Award from Scott & White. (This will certainly teach me a lesson about wearing a hat, especially since my white hair is my best asset.)

More than one hundred business and professional men served as Black Tie Guys on this day! A total of $38,000 was raised for CMN.

Rosebud Roses

Much hard work goes into a show of this caliber, but the rewards are great. Detail is important, and The RoseBud staff was always willing to make us proud. We kept wishing that we could get the ticket price up to at least seventy-five or one hundred dollars because it was definitely worth it. However, we ended this journey on a high note, and the trip was absolutely fantastic.

Anita Perry was a personal friend of Nancy Birdwell, president and CEO of Scott & White Healthcare Foundation, so I now understand how I received such a prestigious award! Thanks, Nancy!

Betty received the Yellow Rose of Texas
Award from Anita Perry in 2002.

SEASONS OF ELEGANCE

The Seasons of Elegance fashion show and luncheon benefitting the Scott & White Children's Hospital took place on Thursday, March 24, 2011, at the Frank W. Mayborn Convention Center in Temple, Texas.

Since my RoseBud was no longer in existence, we decided to feature fabulous fashions from our own closets. I knew where we would find these wonderful clothes that had been purchased from The RoseBud. (Carol Jones wore a few stunning suits from Grace Jones.)

The show took the crowd by storm as Scott & White's Pat Curry roared on stage riding her Harley cycle. She was enthusiastically welcomed by the sell-out crowd.

The celebrity waiters, headed by our Texas Longhorn star, Colt McCoy, included prominent business and professional men from the area. This was an extremely handsome group and the icing on the cake. We are so grateful for this fabulous support. It was such a lovely day to raise funds for a great cause!

My special friend, William E. Horton from Dallas, is an extremely generous man. He graciously offered to professionally decorate the lobby of the Mayborn Center for our event. Bill came into Temple with his van actually loaded with fixtures, mannequins and elaborate fresh flowers and greenery! We were overwhelmed with the results of Bill's gift to us. He created four elaborate storefront windows, each featuring one of four seasons of our year. The mannequins were dressed in exquisite outfits from The RoseBud in years gone by. The massive floral arrangement for each of the windows complemented the ensemble featuring that particular season. I cannot begin to describe the feeling when I laid eyes on this masterpiece! Bill Horton is an angel in our earthly midst! What a splendid gift to celebrate the Children's Hospital in Temple, Texas.

Our own beautiful, talented models paraded up and down the oversized runway in the most elegant fashions imaginable. You know, good fashion is never out of style, and quality is the name of the game. We were entertained with wonderful casual ensembles, day wear and gorgeous formal attire. The accessories were out of this world, and the wraps—coats, shawls, furs—were unbelievable! Yes, there was, as always, something for everyone to admire.

Starfire Designs by Charlie Wharton was a popular gift. The beautiful faceted Mystic Topaz pendant and gold neckwire were won by our precious Sandy Mewhinney. (On the first day of fittings, Sandy wrote a check for $2,500 as a gift to start the ball rolling. Sandy was very popular and a favorite with all who knew her. We were very sad to lose our darling friend, and we will miss her forever. Her sweet husband, Richard Mewhinney, gave Sandy's lovely Starfire pendant to the Contemporaries to auction at their recent fundraiser, Lone Star Nights. Sandy would have been so pleased.)

The committee for Seasons of Elegance was: Karen Lairmore, president, and members Aya Eneli, Sandy Mewhinney, Julie Michaux, Polly Parnell, Monie Roming, Shelley Smith and Martha Tyroch.

When the hospital became a reality, its official name was the McLane Children's Hospital Scott & White. We will forever be grateful to the Drayton McLane family for their extreme love and devotion.

MISTLETOE MOXIE

Christmas was in the air as silver trees hung from the ceiling. Beautiful red, green, gold and silver pine cones in all sizes glittered in all their finery as centers of attraction on snow-white tablecloths with red fluted napkins clasped in brilliant jewels. Chairs were proudly dressed in white covers and sashed in elegant ribbons and ornaments. My, what a sight to behold.

The Contemporaries, supporters of the Azalee Marshall Cultural Activities Center of Temple, were dressed in all their vintage finery right out of their closets. Tiaras were perched on their beautifully coiffed hair, and shiny jewels graced their ears. But the magic touch was the gloves worn to the elbow to finish the perfectly elegant look!

The food for this fundraiser was delicious and professionally served by handsome waiters in black suits, white dress shirts and skinny black ties. Their black snap-brim hats were perfect with their dark sunglasses.

All of this was a tribute to the greatest showband the world could imagine—the Blues Boys from Mississippi. The music was so fabulous that no one could possibly remain in their seats!

All this hard work and attention to detail must be credited to co-chairs Jeannie Wilson and Carla Stanley and the Contemporaries. It was worth every minute of the many hours devoted to make this event among the very best evenings of top-notch entertainment in Temple. And it was all dedicated to benefit the Azalee Marshall Cultural Activities Center in Temple, Texas.

But this is not all this amazing group does for the town. It especially warms my heart to think about all of those precious little children arriving in a caravan of yellow school buses to take an active part in the Contemporaries' Hands-On presentation each year. This event exposes these students to the wonderful world of the arts! If you love kids, this is the perfect place to lend your support.

THE FAMOUS #52 LIPSTICK

The only lip color to grace the models on The RoseBud runway is Yves Saint Laurent (YSL) #52! No other lipstick would do! Number 52 was a perfect blend of pink and orange, producing a natural coral that would complement all skin and hair colors, and it was the only one that would create the right look for all fashion colors and designs.

I am absolutely convinced that makeup is one of the most important accessories in the world of fashion. Coral lipstick and blush bring a clean, fresh, natural look to one's skin—like the face has just been kissed by the sun! A natural made-up face is the greatest asset to one's wardrobe.

I have no tolerance for brown, purple, wine, blue or white lipstick! I am constantly amazed by women who take the magazine ads and fashion designers seriously when they promote such garish looks. In the fashion business, new ideas and colors create reasons for folks to spend money. This is a necessary evil. Without it, stores would go out of business.

When I was helping with S&W's heart calendars, I asked the lady doctors, Ruth Bush and Catherine McNeal, to try the YSL #52 lipstick. I met Ruth, who is a vascular surgeon, in the S&W

hallway one day, and she reached in her scrub jacket and flashed the gold tube of YSL! I loved it!

Catherine is my heart doctor and has modeled for The RoseBud several times. I loved working with these two bright ladies! They are very special!

CLOSING

"Style is a simple way of saying complicated things."

—Jean Cocteau

Patti Thrasher celebrating the Children's Miracle Network.

WHAT IF

How many times in our lives do we say or think to ourselves "what if" I had done something, interpreted something or taken a different course? I have given much thought to how in the world I have reached this time in my life, touched by so many wonderful people and experiences. My exposure has been so enormous!

I think about the folks in my own family and what an impact they had on my life. How could I have not seen this during the early years? I did not really realize just how smart these people were until after I had my fortieth birthday.

I am in my late eighties now, and of course, none of us really knows when our life on earth will end. We do think that life hereafter will be beautiful and more gratifying than we could ever imagine. But—one thing I am certain of is how perfect The RoseBud was. What if I hadn't been blessed with…

…my Uncle Sol and his wisdom.

…my dad's salesmanship and kind heart.

…my Aunt Rose's knowledge of big-city, big-store fashion sense.

…my beautiful mother's contagious laugh and honest desire to serve others.

…my Aunt Johnnye's talents in hairstyling and makeup.

…my precious little sister's teacher compassion.

…my hero brother's way with people and lasting love from all who knew him.

…my dear husband's sincere support in all my many endeavors.

…my customers' sincere loyalty.

…my many supportive acquaintances in the fashion world.

If, if, if! I could go on forever!

I credit all the folks and circumstances listed for my success at The RoseBud! I give special thanks to those who worked alongside me. And, most of all, I praise my hometown of Rosebud, Texas, and the wonderful folks who lived there for watching over all the little kids who called this place home.

The memories are overwhelming. I am now in the twilight years of my life. I have been greatly blessed with two incredible sons, who brought me two very special grandsons and two precious great-grandsons. One of my sweetest gifts is a daughter-in-law whom I adore and consider my best friend. Life is good!

I am having a difficult time ending this book! Every time I think I am finished, another great story pops into my mind, so there really is no end to this story!

My last thought as the book *Rosebud Roses* goes to press is:

If only this great store—with rose-colored carpets, inviting and friendly seating for entertaining customers and friends and lots of fragrant roses in all shades of pink, peach and red—could be complete with my mother greeting all who entered the doors. I am sure she would be serving very hot coffee in elegant china cups!

Every woman would feel the effects of Aunt Pink and her gorgeous creations sewn by the most talented hands in the industry. She was so far ahead of her time. As a little girl, I must have had the most elegant wardrobe of any child. The gorgeous fabrics came from Harry's Place and The Leader, but the creative ideas most certainly came from my Aunt Pink.

Betty's mother and sister on Peggy's wedding day.

THANKS

Looking back on my life, I am very grateful for the many experiences that so often we take for granted. I was a very lucky little girl. I had loving parents, wonderful aunts and uncles, cousins that I adored, a precious little sister who is now a great friend and a little brother who was always my hero and the apple of my eye!

I am a very independent woman who loves people more than things. I am self-sufficient and well able to run my modest household. I am blessed with a husband who willingly assumes his share of duties in our everyday lives. Together, we are a team and know that we can count on each other any time. How rich is this?

I honestly believe that my loved ones in heaven are pleased with me. I feel that my parents, Aunt Rose and Uncle Sol think I have been a respected merchant. I believe Aunt Pink is pleased with my respect for quality fabrics, workmanship and design. As my journey through this life begins to slow just a bit, I thank God for these blessings and hope that I have earned them.

I REMEMBER

As this book goes to press, I will be remembering The RoseBud, a great little store with a big reputation for taking the needs and desires of our customers very seriously. I loved the rose-colored carpets, friendly atmosphere, those wonderful friends and special folks who were our customers. The coffee was always fresh and hot. The cokes were ice cold. The champagne was bubbly. Our doors were open to the public and extremely welcoming to anyone who just came by for a visit.

I find myself looking back on the early years with the priceless exposure to the many talents of my family members. At the time, I had absolutely no idea how lucky I was to have such expert teachers. As a little girl, I must have had the most beautiful clothes of any child. Aunt Pink was the master seamstress, with unlimited designing talents, who created these gorgeous clothes sewn by the most precious hands in the industry. She was so far ahead of her time! The fabulous fabrics she chose came from the piece goods departments of Harry's Place and The Leader, Cruvand's. What a rare jewel this lady was!

Visits with my Uncle Sol were a reason to look forward to Tuesday evenings, when I got to ride in the rumble seat of his immaculate little Model A coupe. We had a standing date for Pal Night at Kirksey's Gem Theater. It really didn't matter what was showing because all the movies were wonderful and everyone in town went to the Gem Theater.

I loved to style Aunt Rose's shiny, long, raven-black hair! I think she also looked forward to these times, when she would talk about how much she loved and appreciated beautiful classic music and good books. She was a class act!

When I remember my parents, I know that I must have been truly blessed! It was obvious how much they loved their children. They were great role models who expected good manners and good morals from us at all times. We lived in a modest house that was the best home anyone could wish for, and we had a sincere respect and appreciation for their sacrifices. The Tapman kids were so lucky!

To be so privileged to live in such an outstanding little town such as Rosebud, Texas, was a gift!

My mother, Tommie, was beautiful clear to the bone. Her skin was flawless, and her silver hair was so enviable. She was smart. She was a great cook. She loved a spotlessly clean house, and she loved her children. It was plain to see that she loved people and had a warm heart. Even though she always worked in the stores, she knew, at all times, where we were and who we were with. She was a strict disciplinarian and could get her message out without laying a hand on us! We adored her! I can honestly say that Peggy, Bubba and I would never want to disappoint her! She was very special!

My dad lived at Canyon Creek Retirement Center after Mother passed away. He loved bringing his new friends by The RoseBud for a visit. He was so proud of the store.

I know that it was a disappointment to my parents that I did not earn a degree from the University of Texas. One thing is for sure. I have orange blood and will be a devoted Longhorn until I die. My loyalty will always be true to The Eyes of Texas.

The world of fashion was exciting and very challenging, but

Rosebud Roses

I loved going to work every day. Many market friends came to visit. They attended our big fashion shows and supported our local fundraisers.

To all our loyal customers, fabulous employees, beautiful and talented models and many friends—it has been a spectacular journey, and along the way, we never forgot to stop and smell the roses!

Thanks for the wonderful memories!

Betty

Daddy (Harry Tapman) and Betty.

ABOUT THE AUTHOR

Betty Thrasher is a first-time author. She shares her thoughts of growing up in a close-knit family in the small Central Texas town of Rosebud. She always felt that she was destined to own a very special business featuring teaching and pleasing more than selling. She named her ladies' boutique after the town that captured her heart through the gifts received from the wonderful people who lived there.

The RoseBud was a positive reflection of her family's businesses. Her best years were spent in this special business located in Exchange Plaza, Temple, Texas.

AWARDS AND HONORS

1. The Village of Canyon Creek Volunteer Service Award 1987.
2. Served on Baylor University's Family & Consumer Sciences Board 1998–2006
3. Wildflower Country Club Board of Directors.
4. Junior League of Bell County Community Partner Award 1998.
5. Temple Mayor's Proclamation called November 7, 1996, "Betty Thrasher Day," courtesy of Altrusa.
6. VA Women's Club Benefit Award 1996.
7. Scott & White Auxiliary Award for Spectacular Service: Ten Years, 1993–2003
8. City Federation of Women's Clubs, Temple, Outstanding Community Volunteer 2000.
9. Historic Waco Presentation Award 2002.
10. Rosebud High School Outstanding Alumnus Award 2002.
11. Scott & White Hospital Service Award for Twenty Years, 2002.
12. Yellow Rose of Texas Award, presented by First Lady Anita Perry on September 27, 2002.
13. Temple Mayor's Proclamation called August 29, 2007, "Betty Thrasher Day," courtesy of the Contemporaries.

14. Served on the Advisory Board of the Dallas International Apparel Mart for several years.
15. Haddasa Award.
16. Girl Scout Woman of Distinction Award 2013.

Betty was invited to help organize the Scott & White Visionaries—a group of philanthropic women who stage fundraisers for McLane Children's Hospital, Scott & White.

Betty belongs to the Contemporaries of the Azalee Marshall Cultural Activities Center in Temple. Until this year, she was a member of the Federated Women's Clubs of Temple, Texas. Betty is an honorary member of Altrusa International, Temple, Texas.

Betty's mother and sister on Peggy's wedding day.

THANKS

Looking back on my life, I am very grateful for the many experiences that so often we take for granted. I was a very lucky little girl. I had loving parents, wonderful aunts and uncles, cousins that I adored, a precious little sister who is now a great friend and a little brother who was always my hero and the apple of my eye!

I am a very independent woman who loves people more than things. I am self-sufficient and well able to run my modest household. I am blessed with a husband who willingly assumes his share of duties in our everyday lives. Together, we are a team and know that we can count on each other any time. How rich is this?

I honestly believe that my loved ones in heaven are pleased with me. I feel that my parents, Aunt Rose and Uncle Sol think I have been a respected merchant. I believe Aunt Pink is pleased with my respect for quality fabrics, workmanship and design. As my journey through this life begins to slow just a bit, I thank God for all these blessings and hope that I have earned them.